The Sociology of Identity

The Sociology of Identity

Authenticity, Multidimensionality, and Mobility

Wayne H. Brekhus

polity

The right of Wayne H. Brekhus to be identified as Author of this Work has been asserted in accordance with the UK Copyright, Designs and Patents Act 1988.

First published in 2020 by Polity Press

Polity Press
65 Bridge Street
Cambridge CB2 1UR, UK

Polity Press
101 Station Landing
Suite 300
Medford, MA 02155, USA

ISBN-13: 978-1-5095-3480-7
ISBN-13: 978-1-5095-3481-4(pb)

A catalogue record for this book is available from the British Library.

Library of Congress Cataloging-in-Publication Data
Names: Brekhus, Wayne, author.
Title: The sociology of identity : authenticity, multidimensionality, and
    mobility / Wayne H. Brekhus.
Description: Cambridge, UK ; Medford, MA : Polity Press, 2020. | Includes
    bibliographical references and index. | Summary: "A lively exploration
    of the self through the social"-- Provided by publisher.
Identifiers: LCCN 2020012852 (print) | LCCN 2020012853 (ebook) | ISBN
    9781509534807 (hardback) | ISBN 9781509534814 (paperback) | ISBN
    9781509534821 (epub)
Subjects: LCSH: Group identity. | Identity (Psychology)--Social aspects.
Classification: LCC HM753 .B74 2020 (print) | LCC HM753 (ebook) | DDC
    305--dc23
LC record available at https://lccn.loc.gov/2020012852
LC ebook record available at https://lccn.loc.gov/2020012853

Typeset in 11 on 13 pt Sabon by
Servis Filmsetting Ltd, Stockport, Cheshire
Printed and bound in Great Britain by CPI Group (UK) Ltd, Croydon

For further information on Polity, visit our website: politybooks.com.

Contents

Acknowledgments

I would like to thank Jonathan Skerrett at Polity for encouraging this project and for his supportive advice throughout the process, from idea to proposal to publication. I am also grateful to the three anonymous reviewers for their helpful suggestions on a first draft of the manuscript. I thank Manuela Tecusan for her very attentive and thorough copy-editing of the manuscript.

Eviatar Zerubavel's passion for thinking about big topics in analytically creative ways continues to inspire my own thinking. I am grateful for his ongoing enthusiasm and intellectual guidance. I thank Lorenzo Sabetta for the many stimulating conversations we have had on issues related to identity and the unmarked. He came from Italy to study with me for a year, as a postdoctoral fellow, and I am indebted to him for our friendship. I also thank Jay Gubrium for our many interesting discussions about identity and for his encouragement as a colleague. I thank my wife Rachel, who has helped me think through ideas, has read through and commented on drafts and revisions, and has been a tremendous source of intellectual and moral support.

Introduction

Identity is central to human meaning, social life, and social interaction. We often think of identity as a personal, individual matter, but identity is intensely social both in its formation and in its implications. Identity has important consequences for how we organize our lives, wield social power, include and exclude others from our closest social networks, and produce and reproduce privilege and marginality. We do identity for a variety of reasons, some tacit, some strategic. We express identity in both individual and collective forms. This book examines the sociology of identity, emphasizing three themes: authenticity, multidimensionality, and mobility. These themes are intricately tied to power, privilege, stigma, marginality, and the politics of inclusion and exclusion. They also directly relate to one another. We strive toward authenticity to ourselves and to our categories of belonging in multidimensional, fluid, and mobile ways.

Authenticity refers to the ways in which people try to authenticate personal selves or group membership. *Multidimensionality* refers to how people navigate multiple intersecting elements that make up their self-identity or collective identity. *Mobility* refers to the strategies and cultural currencies people use to navigate transitory and migratory shifts in their selves or in their collective identities across space and time. These organizing themes bring together a diverse body of research on identities to specifically highlight the important social work that identity does. The social work that identity does is both positive and negative, ranging from pride to prejudice, from altruism to bullying, from finding belonging to differentiating.

Identity is a concept directly connected to one of sociology's central concerns: the production and reproduction of social inequalities. In consequence, the approach developed here differs from approaches in texts that regard identity as a primarily personal concern, connected to individual psychology, or that examine it largely as a matter of self-conception. Individualistic approaches often assume a general self not directly tied to sociological, cultural, and material dimensions that differentially shape different social types of selves. Psychological approaches focused on the self are important in their own right, but the romantic image of an individual looking in a mirror and wondering "Who am I?"—even when presented as a "looking-glass self" (Cooley 1964) that considers the question by internalizing society—puts before us a relatively individualistic view of identity that misses some of its dynamic social nature. The concepts of authenticity, multidimensionality, and mobility help us to see the complex social work that identity does. Related to the fundamentally social character of identity, this book examines identity in collective as well as socially shaped individual forms. To begin thinking about identity, let us consider the following examples.

In Italy, Mahmood (Alessandro Mahmoud), a 26-year-old man born in Milan to a mother from Sardinia and a father from Egypt, captured the hearts of audiences at a televised singing competition in 2019. Mahmood became an instant pop sensation, winning Italy's San Remo music festival, and thus qualified to represent Italy at the 2019 Eurovision song contest in Tel Aviv, Israel. But the victory that allowed Mahmood to represent Italy turned out to be controversial. Italian anti-immigrant political leaders expressed anger that Mahmood was selected by the judges and that he beat out singers of "more Italian" songs. Deputy Prime Minister Matteo Salvini tweeted: "#Mahmood ... meh ... the most beautiful Italian song?!?"—a line that many interpreted as a challenge to the Italian identity of Mahmood and his music. In response to the controversy, a member of Salvini's political party introduced legislation designed to limit "foreign" music played on the radio. For Mahmood's critics, his partially Egyptian ancestry made the authenticity of his Italian identity suspect; his Egyptian heritage weighed on their perceptions of his identity. In response to these attacks on his identity, Mahmood identified himself as one hundred percent Italian. The deputy prime minister and members of his party implied that Mahmood's multiethnic background gave him a "foreign" and diluted form of Italianness, which was less authentic that that of someone of "pure Italian descent." Mahmood, by contrast, saw nothing in his multidimensional ethnic ancestry that diluted his authenticity or rendered him anything but one hundred percent Italian.

In California, a working-class Mexican American teenage girl puts on dark lip color and dark nail polish before she heads to high school. She prefers the dark colors popular in her *las chicas* social clique, a group of mostly working-class Latina girls who define themselves against the popular clique of preppie girls or "preps." Across town, in an upper-middle-class neighborhood, her white classmate, a prep girl, is putting on the light pastel lip and nail colors favored in her social clique. The Latina girl deliberately chooses a dark lip color popular in her social network; she wants to set herself apart from the dominant preps, who are mostly white (see Bettie 2000, 2014). In doing so she shares with her "cliquemates" a subcultural style that emphasizes their marked ethnicity and their working-class status. She also chooses darker colors associated with "somberness, age, and sophistication," colors that lack the "youth, innocence, and gaiety" associations of the pastel colors preferred in the preppie clique; such color choices coincide respectively with working- and middle-class life-stage expectations (see Bettie 2000: 14–15). The white middle-class girl who wears light pastel lipstick also wears relatively expensive clothes, in a fashionable style approved by her peers in the school's most popular clique. In this way she performs a school-sanctioned femininity, which expresses her identity as a socially valued "good" white kid from a middle-class background, and she distinguishes herself from the more socially marked "deviant" subcultures of the school. She perceives girls who wear dark makeup as "less classy" (and lower in social class) and regards her own performance as more respectable than theirs.

In Nottingham, England, a middle-aged and middle-class man with British citizenship identifies as European and wants the United Kingdom to remain in the European Union. Across the city a working-class man of a similar age identifies as British and strongly supports Brexit—Britain's exit from the European Union. Both men live in the United Kingdom, but one identifies as British and European and the other as British. These differences in identification correspond to significant differences in worldviews and political attitudes.

In the United States Sarah Palin, vice presidential candidate in 2008, generated controversy by stating that "the best of America is in these small towns that we get to visit, and in these wonderful pockets of what I call the real America . . . hard working, very patriotic, very pro-America areas of this great nation" (Silver 2008). Palin made it forcefully clear that she aligns herself with a popular conservative view that the most authentic, "real American" identity lies in the predominantly white small towns and rural areas of the American Midwest, of the American South, and of the Great Plains and Rocky Mountain states. Other politicians and cultural commentators pushed back, emphasizing a "real America" that welcomes immigrants and is multicultural or culturally cosmopolitan, diverse, and urban. A strong debate ensued over the identities of "America" and "Americans" and over who counts as "authentically American" and where. This debate rages on as Donald Trump's nostalgic, nativist vision of "making America great again" clashes with the more anti-nostalgic, pro-immigrant, multicultural visions of American greatness touted by his critics, in a hotly divided country torn between opposing visions of its desired identity and of what counts most for a definition of authentic Americanness.

These are all examples that illustrate the social nature and the importance of identity. Identity is a vital organizing element of social life. We use it to construct meaning, to classify, to articulate sameness and difference, to include and to exclude, to confer status and to assign stigma. Identity shapes how we categorize one another and how we interpret the world. We manage and construct our own identities and we are active in the construction and labeling of others' identities. We construct identity at both the individual and the collective level. These examples also point to the three central themes related to identity that I mentioned at the beginning: authenticity, multidimensionality, and mobility.

The controversy over whether or not pop star Mahmood's music qualifies as Italian revolves around competing definitions of what it takes for something to count toward an authentic national identity. Similarly, in the United States heated debates over where the "real America" lies center on contested definitions of authenticity. Self-identified Brits and self-identified Europeans have conflicting ideas about their identities as residents of the United Kingdom; and they, too, get into disputes over national identity and authenticity. Italians, residents of the United States, and residents of the United Kingdom alike have ideas about the authenticity of their and others' claims to a national identity.

Questions of authenticity are complex, intersectional, and multidimensional. When California high school students choose their lipstick, they are not only concerned with belonging to their group of friends but relatedly interested in backing their claims to subcultural status through expressions of self and subcultural authenticity. By dressing so as to convey subcultural identity, high school girls simultaneously do race, class, gender, and sexuality. When Mahmood suggests that he is one hundred percent Italian, he constructs an Italian identity that is expressed through his ethnicity, his gender, and his sexuality and that combines his Italian and Egyptian parental lineages. His complex intersectional claim to Italian authenticity is challenged by politicians who demand a more restrictive, more "pure," and less intersectional ethnic expression of Italian identity.

Identity is also mobile and fluid. What it means to be an Italian or an American is a shifting terrain, which influences individual claims to identity as well as perceptions of national identity. The contested definition of "real American" people and places occurs in a shifting demographic landscape wherein authenticity claims based on demographics from the 1950s are challenged partly on the basis of the empirical realities of the demographics of the 2020s. Just as national identities are fluid, individual identities, too, are mobile and changing.

These themes of authenticity, multidimensionality, and mobility will return throughout the book. Every theme will be discussed in separate chapters, but each one also relates to the others. People navigate authenticity by ordering their multidimensional aspects and by deploying multiple dimensions in a mobile fashion across space and time.

What Is Identity?

What exactly is identity? A precise definition of this term is hard to come by. No single formula adequately encompasses the range of ways in which the concept is used in the social sciences or in everyday life. Identity can be understood both as something that is relatively fixed and essential and as something malleable and fluid. It can be regarded as something deeply etched or as something that appears at the surface. The etymon of the term "identity" is the Latin pronoun *idem, eadem, idem* ("same"), which suggests that an important component of its meaning is a degree of sameness across a category that it conveys (see Jenkins 1996: 3; Lawler 2008: 2). At the same time identity also implies an individual's uniqueness and difference from all others (Lawler 2008: 2). Tensions between sameness and difference illustrate the complexities of identity and require us to appreciate and understand the nuances in how identity is understood, assigned, claimed, enacted, and deployed. The contradiction between sameness and difference is often played out in identity–authenticity claims. When making claims of authenticity vis-à-vis an identity category, individuals often emphasize their similarity to other members of that category—ways in which they are, say, like other Italians, Texans, Christians, distance runners, alcoholics, vegetarians, gun owners, abuse survivors, or soldiers. Yet when they make claims of "self-authenticity" individuals often highlight their distinctiveness from others. In group identification, individuals often emphasize their similarities to other in-group members, while when it comes to self-identification they consider personal uniqueness a first priority.

One challenge to the study of identity is that the term is used in a wide variety of ways by different scholars. Many scholars take a personal and individual approach, looking at *personal identity* or *self-identity* as the feature that individually differentiates one person from others. Other scholars are interested primarily in *social identity* and the ways in which individuals internalize collective categorial identifications (see Jenkins 2014: 114). And still others who are interested in collective categorial identifications want to understand not only how individuals internalize them but how collectives and non-individual social forms such as nations, schools, neighborhoods, and organizations also have their own *collective identities*. To understand identity it is thus important to recognize that it can refer to self-identity, to social identity, or to collective identity. Although analysts separate these different forms of identity to demonstrate the multiple layers of the concept, such forms are often intertwined in everyday life. That is, collective and social identities influence personal identity and, likewise, personal and social identifications factor into collective identities.

In arguing against the concept of identity, Brubaker and Cooper (2000) make the point that the term has multiple meanings. Identity, they argue, is a concept distinct from interest. Interests are instrumental and have a clear goal, while actions related to identity have meaning-oriented rather than instrumental goals. Identity, in one reading, designates how action—individual or collective—is governed by particular self-understandings rather than by universal self-interest (Brubaker and Cooper 2000: 6). When understood as a collective phenomenon, it indicates an important sameness among members of a social category; when understood as a product of social or political action, it sheds light on the interactive development of the kinds of collective identifications and self-understandings that make identity politics and collective political action possible. For Brubaker and Cooper, the sheer number of uses of the concept of identity makes it analytically fragmented and unusable as a concept. They assert, for example, that, "if one wants to argue that particularistic self-understandings shape social and political action in a non-instrumental manner, one can simply say so . . . If one wants to examine the meanings and significance people give to constructs such as 'race,' 'ethnicity,' and 'nationality . . . it is not clear what one gains by aggregating them under the flattening rubric of identity" (Brubaker and Cooper 2000: 6). Brubaker and Cooper point to the widely different, and sometimes diverging, uses of identity and assert that this variety makes the concept unusable.

According to the two authors, combining race, ethnicity, nationality, and other social constructions under the single rubric of identity brings little gain. This provocative statement is important—not because it precludes the study of identity, but rather because it requires us to be explicit about the analytic benefits of a unifying rubric such as identity. There is in fact much to be gained by studying such different collective identifications as race, ethnicity, nationality, gender, sexuality, and subculture for their analytic similarities and to look at self-identity, collective identity, and the identity of non-individual forms searching for parallel processes of identity construction and identity marking and unmarking. Here, rather than seeing race, ethnicity, nationality, gender, sexuality, subculture, and other constructs as too dissimilar to be studied together, we can acknowledge their substantive differences while still valuing their formal, general analytic similarities. The ways in which people navigate social constructs to organize their self-definitions, to generalize about others, and to participate in the boundary politics of inclusion and exclusion are worth studying not only in their separate, individual substantive areas or in their separate and specific uses (e.g. personal identification, collective mobilization), but for analytic similarities and tensions between them across domains and uses.

In this book I analyze the broad range of categories around which we construct identities. Although identity is diverse in its forms, the latter are often similar in their organization and in their general analytic qualities. I therefore bring together the insights of symbolic interactionist ethnographic studies on particular types of identity with the analytic advantages of a cognitive sociological approach that identifies general patterns through comparisons across specific forms.

Cognitive Sociology Meets Symbolic Interactionism: Social Pattern Analysis of Identity Authenticity, Multidimensionality, and Mobility

To synthesize a wide range of sociological conceptions of identity and to compare identity across the many substantive forms and purposes in which it expresses itself, I follow Eviatar Zerubavel's (2007) *social pattern analysis*—a concept-driven cognitive sociology approach to general sociological theorizing. This kind of formal sociological theorizing is characterized by lack of interest in singularity and in isolating unique phenomena and by a concern with cross-case, cross-level, and cross-phenomenal comparisons. Zerubavel (forthcoming) argues that, in contrast to more substantively oriented types of scholarship, such as historical or descriptive ethnographic work, a formal sociological analysis transcends the specific and the concrete in order to focus on general and abstract commonalities. Social pattern analysis is a concept-driven sociology that illuminates *sensitizing concepts* (see Zerubavel 2007). I combine this general formal theoretical approach, however, with specific, empirically interesting micro-sociological cases of identity enactments and performances studied by symbolic interactionist ethnographers. I draw significantly on ethnographic researchers who study specific identities, roles, and groups, because the concepts they develop in specific settings such as punk authenticity (Force 2009), or black cultural capital (Carter 2003), or protean racial identities (Rockquemore and Brunsma 2002) are analytically applicable to other kinds of settings and generalizable to other kinds of cases. Applying social pattern analysis to punk authenticity and black cultural capital, for instance, allows us to extend insights from these specific types to other kinds of authenticities and cultural capital. Here I apply the general theoretical concerns of social pattern analysis to theoretically focused ethnographies that are analytically portable, speak to larger macro-level issues, and build upon other ethnographies and research studies (see Fine 2003).

The three major, sensitizing concepts labeled in this book "identity authenticity," "identity multidimensionality," and "identity mobility," which I use to frame an understanding of the sociology of identities, are general theoretical concepts that demonstrate analytic commonalities and generic formal similarities across very different kinds of identity. These concepts are important for understanding the power dimensions of identity and the role of identity constructions in producing and reproducing inequalities, marginality, and privilege. In the course of exploring these three properties of identity, other analytic concepts will also be highlighted and discussed in connection to their broader relevance to the sociology of identity. Those analytic concepts have developed in the specific contexts of sociological ethnographies and identity literatures, but they apply across different types of identity.

Bringing together theoretical traditions to analyze the sociology of identity is an ambitious task, particularly given that the term "identity" is used in multiple ways by analysts. Rather than provide a single definition of identity, my goal is to present identity and identification in the pluralistic ways that they are employed by social actors and described by social analysts and to explain the interactional and social boundary work that identity does. This means that the text will move between relatively thin, weak forms of identification and thick, strong forms of identity, between the conscious use of categorial identities as strategic resources and the unconscious expression of them as a tacit presentation that does work (even when what it does goes largely unacknowledged), and between expressions of self-identity and group identity. The concepts of authenticity, multidimensionality, and mobility will be explored through a cognitive sociological lens, illustrating how these concepts relate to one another and to the ways in which we interactionally perform identity. Organization around these themes and around the key concepts that cut across theoretical perspectives in identity studies provides an overview designed to spark new insights and fresh ideas for exploring the stakes of identity. An emphasis on how these themes relate among themselves and to social inequalities further frames why identity is an important topic for sociological study.

Why Study Identity in Sociology?

Why should sociologists study identity? Answering this question relates both to why they should concern themselves with something that is already extensively studied in psychology and to why they should examine the seemingly personal issue of identity rather than the big structural questions that drive much of the sociological research.

People often think of identity as a very personal, unique, and individual thing. Given individualist notions of identity and our cultural tendency to think in terms of personal identities first, psychologists have typically been regarded as the identity specialists. Just as economists study the economy and political scientists study politics, psychologists are well suited to studying human personalities and an individual's sense of self. Sociologists have a significant role to play, however, as identities are fundamentally social. We construct, negotiate, and narrate our selves in social networks and cultural contexts. Identities have important consequences for how we live our lives and whom we include in or exclude from our social networks. Identities shift and change as we move from one setting to the next; we respond to the cultural influences and cultural audiences of different social and geographic sites of performance. The salience of competing attributes changes across settings and across the life course according to our experiences and the people we interact with. Identities are heavily tied to social power and to privilege and marginalization. Understanding identity therefore requires examining the social complexity of identities in their multiple social forms and in the varied social and cultural uses they are put to.

Sociologists often study big-picture aggregate issues and large-scale social problems. The massive issues of social inequality, globalization, migration, environment and environmental change, education, political systems, and organizations are central to the concerns of contemporary sociologists. On the surface, identity can appear like an interesting micro-sociological issue, but one that may not be integral to the really big issues of our time. This is a perception perhaps shaped in part by earlier, more individualist strands of symbolic interactionist theories of identity and by the initial political stance of the Society for the Study of Symbolic Interaction, which presented its interests in the local and interactional as a challenge to mainstream sociology and to its wider emphases. While the study of identity has traditionally attracted micro-level sociologists of everyday life (in the tradition of Erving Goffman) and symbolic interactionists (in the traditions of Mead, Blumer, and Cooley), identity is not limited to those interested in self-presentation and symbolic interaction. Identity is also relevant for many of the big issues.

Take for instance the strongly nationalist political cultural and turns now current in the United States, the United Kingdom, Brazil, and Italy. These movements may form around big issues such as immigration, the economy, resource allocation, organizations, crime and criminal justice, race, and class; but they are also—and intensely—about identity. They are both about the individuals' perceptions of self-identity and about constructions of national and ethnic identities. Even the problem of gun access, an especially prominent topic in the United States, is significantly tied to identity, as owners of concealed carry guns often construct for themselves moral identities that are tied to tacit assumptions about the race, class, and masculinity of "good guys with guns" and about who needs protection and who falls outside the boundary (Stroud 2012, 2015). In a multicultural, globalizing world in which prominent issues of inclusion and exclusion appear in a wide variety of forms—for example, in immigration debates and controversies, in the British Brexit vote to exit the European Union, or in the rise of white nationalist identity politics in the United States and Europe—issues of identity are pushed to the forefront of sociological interest and concern. Identity provides a mechanism through which we can understand macro phenomena.

About the Book

Identity is a central component of social life. It is the basic cognitive mechanism that people use to sort themselves, individually and collectively (Jenkins 2014). It helps us to develop a sense of who we are, how we relate to others, and how we make sense of the world. It is used to confer status and to mark stigma—in a word, to establish social positioning (Campion 2019).

Identities are socially and culturally constructed and are negotiated in complex, multidimensional ways. Their complexity is tied to cognitive and interactional dimensions of sociocultural privilege and marginalization. Multidimensional identities are constructed in both collective and individual forms, and privilege and marginalization are also negotiated both collectively and individually. Performing and defining the authenticity of one's identity, emphasizing the multiple dimensions of one's self or category, and shifting identities in a mobile fashion across space and time are just some of the ways in which complex identities are negotiated.

This book will orient readers to sociological approaches to understanding social identity, placing particular emphasis on concepts and ideas that arise from the sociological study of identity. While there has been much literature on self-identity from psychological, social psychological, and developmental perspectives, and while studies concerning the self, the social role, and the status of individuals have been ongoing, this book emphasizes identity as an inherently social phenomenon. The primary focus here is on the sociology of social identities rather than on the psychology of the self or on the experimental psychology and social psychology of self-identities. I will introduce and synthesize cultural, qualitative, and interactionist sociological approaches to the topic, emphasizing the complex social and intersectional nature of identities. The book is organized both around social influences on multidimensional self-identities and around collective identities of social forms other than individuals. In advancing a social and sociological concept of identity, I will highlight new and emerging notions of identity, while also calling attention to the foundational roots of more recent developments.

What is the nature of the self? How do we negotiate multiple identities? Is identity achieved or ascribed, self-appointed or other-defined? How do we construct boundaries of inclusion and exclusion through identity? How do power and privilege, oppression and stigma factor into identity? How do we negotiate multiple identities? How do identities shift from one setting to another? What is the role of place in constructing identity? How do cultural categories and patterns of cognitive attention and inattention shape identities? How is identity influenced by and managed through new technologies? How is identity mobile and fluid in a fast-paced, globalizing, multidimensional world? How do ethnocentrism and cosmopolitanism affect self-identity and collective identities? These are some of the questions that the present book will explore.

As a sociological account, the interactional accomplishment of identity in response to social settings and to cultural influences will be a significant focus. Identity is fluid, and it is negotiated, accomplished, and reaccomplished in social environments and cultural settings. Rather than focusing on it as something static and essential, I will place an emphasis here on the symbolic interactionist idea that identity develops through our relational interactions with others. With their notion of "doing difference," West and Fenstermaker (1995) advance an understanding of difference as an ongoing interactional accomplishment. They build on West and Zimmerman's (1987) conceptualization of gender as a routine, methodical, and ongoing accomplishment achieved through perceptual, interactional, and micro-political activities, to argue that, as organizing categories of social difference, gender, race, and class are all interactional accomplishments as well as comparable mechanisms for producing social inequality. West and Fenstermaker focus on race, class, and gender, but their approach is broadly relevant to categories of social difference. A sociological conception of identity is informed both by an interest in the social accomplishment of difference and identity and by a concern with how the accomplishment of difference (and of sameness) plays into the politics of exclusion and inclusion and produces and reproduces social inequalities. Combining interactional understandings of doing difference with cognitive sociological understandings of how we negotiate authenticity, multidimensionality, and mobility through the deployment and code-switching of marked (socially salient) and unmarked (socially taken-for-granted) attributes is a key element in this approach. The overall argument is that identities are socially created and negotiated (1) by performing, constructing, and navigating authenticity; (2) by balancing multiple attributes of privilege and marginalization; and (3) by deploying identity in a mobile, flexible, and fluid fashion across space and time. Identity is a strategic resource for negotiating boundaries and for managing power relations at both the individual and the collective level.

The material is organized as follows.

In chapter 1 I introduce and discuss major sociological traditions in the study of social identity. These traditions are symbolic interactionism, Goffman's dramaturgical sociology, Bourdieu's theory of dispositional habits, modernity and postmodernity traditions, feminist standpoint theories such as intersectional analyses, and cultural cognitive symbolic boundaries traditions. Introducing these multiple approaches will serve to demonstrate the scope of theoretical research that explores the social and cultural dimensions of identities and to show how these traditions complement one another in painting a picture of the dynamic social character of identities. At the same time, these very traditions constitute a range of approaches that can inform one another and enhance our conceptual and empirical understanding of the sociology of identities. The various approaches presented in chapter 1 can be brought into greater overlap and dialogue with one another to explicate our understanding of social identities as collective, complex, and multidimensional; and the unifying themes of authenticity, multidimensionality, and mobility cut across the variety of traditions.

In chapter 2 I look beyond the individual, to discuss the many collective forms that identity takes. Identity is constructed not only in individuals but in collective social forms as well. Nations, communities, social movements, subcultures, families, generations, professions, and organizations form and build identities and have identities attributed to them by others. This chapter emphasizes several forms of collective identity. Examples include national identities, subcultural identities, social movement identities, city identities, neighborhood identities, organizational identities, and ethnic and racial category identities. These examples will highlight non-individual ways in which we construct identity. Key concepts discussed in the chapter will be collective identity, the identity of collective social forms, imagined communities, social movement identity, organizational identity, place identity, and communities of belonging.

Chapter 3 looks at identity boundary work and negotiations of authenticity. Performing and defining the authentication of one's identity are two of the ways in which we erect boundaries of inclusion and exclusion and boundaries of belonging and not belonging. Analyzing the authenticity of identity across a range of contexts and across different levels of analysis highlights ongoing issues of boundary building and maintenance. The chapter will explore authenticity, authenticity disputes, symbolic belonging, and inclusion and exclusion work across a range of identity contexts, demonstrating that collective and individual performances of authenticity are an important part of identity boundary maintenance and exclusion. Key concepts addressed are identity authenticity, self-authenticity, "false" and "true" selves, group authenticity, negotiating identity, subcultural capital, identity disputes, contested identities, ethnic fraud, and ethnic authenticity.

How do we negotiate multiple identities? How do power, privilege, and marginality intersect and shape the presentation of identity and the patterns of inclusion and exclusion? In chapter 4 I will focus on the multidimensionality and intersectionality of self-identities and collective identities. Intersectional analysis in the sociology of identity draws on foundational traditions in feminist standpoint theories (e.g. Smith 1987; Crenshaw 1991; King 1988; Hill Collins 2009) as well as on "social mindscape" cognitive sociological traditions (see Zerubavel 1997; Brekhus 2007), which in turn explore Simmel's (1969) interest in webs of intersecting identity affiliations and multiple standpoints. While social interactionist perspectives emphasize the social nature of identity by locating it within the social context, social standpoint intersectional perspectives add to our understanding of the social nature of identity by introducing social power and *social location*. Social location refers to the position where the demographic and social characteristics of a person, a social group, or a community place them within a status hierarchy. Our social selves are composed of competing group and demographic attributes, which correspond to different forms of politics of inclusion and exclusion and to various degrees of privilege and stigma. Modern identity scholarship is increasingly interested in the multidimensional character of identities, especially as this multidimensionality relates to social inequalities. Chapter 4 will highlight this property of identity and the negotiation between unmarked normative privilege and marked, accented marginality in identities, examining the multiple influences on identities and the interactional presentations of multidimensionality. Key concepts featuring there will be multidimensionality, intersectionality, social standpoint, marked difference, accented particularization, non-inclusive universalization, unmarked privilege, and the interactional reproduction of social inequalities.

The fundamentally social nature of identity means that it is not only complex and multifaceted, as is modern social life itself; it is also fluid and shifting in a multicontextual world. Identity is a multidimensional resource deployed across a plurality of social contexts. In chapter 5 I will look at how multidimensional identities are mobile and transitory across time and space and are deployed as shifting resources by the multifaceted social actor. Identity is mobile and individuals can draw upon context and specific forms of cultural capital, which are valued as identity currencies in some settings and devalued in other settings. The chapter highlights the strategic deployment of identity across time and space, emphasizing the mobile, fluid nature of multiple identities. The previous concepts of identity authenticity and multidimensionality, addressed in chapters 3 and 4, are here understood in relation to the ways in which we use time and space to organize authenticity and multidimensionality. Key concepts discussed here are identity mobility, fluidity, identity currencies, place-based identities, and temporal identities.

In the conclusion I focus on the relationships between identity authenticity, multidimensionality, and mobility, discuss research that reflects on and elaborates on these relationships, and invite you, the reader, to examine your own identities and the social groups that forge them.

1

Sociological Approaches to Identity

Identity has become a central concept in modern sociological thought. Introduced to sociology in 1902 by Cooley (1964) and developed in 1934 by Mead (Mead and Morris 1967), who saw identity as important to the self-concept and to the self as shaped by interactions with others, the idea of socially influenced self-identities represents a sociological approach to understanding this entity—the self. In his foundational work on the social nature of self-identity, Mead argues that selves or self-identities emerge from interactions with others and through social experience. We learn to perceive ourselves and to adjust our own self-under-standings through dialogue and interaction with others. Mead, building on Cooley, Thomas, and the pragmatist tradition in the social sciences, is widely acknowledged as the founding figure in the theoretical tradition of thinking sociologically about the self. Drawing upon Erikson's (1994) popularization of the concept of identity in psychology, Goffman (1959, 1986) and Stone (1962) more directly introduced the concept of social identity to sociology in the late 1950s and early 1960s and demonstrated that identity is situated in social relations, social interactions, and encounters. Traditions in the study of identity that derive from Cooley, Mead, and, later, Goffman and Stone focused primarily on the individual and on how interpersonal interactions shape the formation of the self; perspectives emphasizing the individual dominated identity research in sociology through the 1970s (Cerulo 1997).

Since the 1980s, sociological research on identities has increasingly focused not just on the self as a source of identity, but on collective identities. Cerulo (1997: 386) notes that this shift is fueled by three important trends:

(1) Social and nationalist movements have increased scholarly interest in issues of group agency and political action, paying particular attention to the political implications of collective definitions around race, ethnicity, class, gender, and sexuality.
(2) Intellectual concerns with agency and self-direction have enhanced the study of identification processes and how category distinctions are created, maintained, and changed.
(3) New communication technologies have diminished the importance of physical co-presence and expanded the array of generalized others one interacts with in constructing their identities.

Spurred on by an interest in understanding collective identities as the product of differentiation and social boundary making, sociologists of identity have returned to their collectivist roots, while still maintaining symbolic interactionist concerns with the interactional performance of boundaries and identities.

The nature of collective thought and the "we-ness" of collectives have generated a longstanding interest among sociologists, ever since Durkheim's preoccupation with the relationship between the mental and the social was expressed in his idea of a "collective conscience." In Durkheim's view, the self and the mind are socially constructed through their dynamic relationship with the social rather than constituted in an individual's relationship with the natural environment (Brekhus 2015: 5). Similarly, Marx's idea of class consciousness—the idea that people observe the world from a social standpoint, which is that of their own social class, with its specific life experiences and identifications—reflects an interest, now classical, in the shared understandings of collectives. Modern sociologists of identity have focused more directly on cultural and social expressions of we-ness as collective identities. But perhaps the classical sociologist whose ideas about the relationship between role and social identity have most influenced contemporary thinking is Simmel. In the "web of group affiliations," Simmel (1969: 140–3) perceives the individual personality as formed by one's multiple intersecting group affiliations. Individuals internalize their various affiliations of belonging, thus creating a self that is formed by the many intersecting group cultures they belong to. They develop a multiply networked worldview and social standpoint. Thus, for Simmel, the individual is shaped by the intersecting collectives that he or she internalizes. Simmel's ideas reflect a sociological interest in intersectional identities and in the multidimensionality of identities. As we will see in chapter 4, the concept of intersectionality (the idea that race, class, and gender intersect in shaping the identities and experiences of working-class black women, middle-class Latina women, and other multiply located individuals), currently popular in identity and inequality studies, shares analytic similarities with the concept of overlapping affiliations, which Simmel was interested in.

Unlike Simmel, who placed a broad emphasis on roles, modern intersectionality theorists focus more directly on affiliations tied to inequality and power, for example race, class, gender, and sexuality; yet the formal dimensions of how intersecting affiliations make identities multidimensional are similar. Hughes (1945) brings out the power dimension of intersecting group attributes in individuals, in developing the concept of a *master status* for those roles or identities that overpower other characteristics in defining social expectations about someone. Hughes identifies race for black people in the United States as one of these master status-defining traits that a black person carries into any social context. Noting that professional standing is also a powerful characteristic, Hughes highlights the intersectional dilemma faced by black professionals who simultaneously hold a stigmatized racial master status (negro in the United States of the 1940s) and a privileged professional status (doctor). Hughes's concept of the master status as a salient social standpoint, together with his observations about the intersections of different salient statuses (some stigmatizing, some privileging), is foundational to modern approaches that examine the power dimensions of intersecting collective identities as experienced and internalized by individuals.

As we can see from the varying classical sociological influences, the study of identity is a broad theoretical field, with multiple foci. The concept of identity can be used in very different ways—which stem from different theoretical traditions—to refer to widely varying forms of identity such as personal identity, social identity, or collective identity. Making sense of these multiple traditions and how they interrelate is an important task. To do that, I discuss several theoretical traditions in the sociology of identity. Some of these traditions speak directly to one another, in an integrative scholarly conversation, while others have developed independently and are distinct from one another. The purpose of introducing these multiple approaches is both to show the scope of different, primarily qualitative sociological research traditions that explore the social and cultural dimensions of identities and to demonstrate how these traditions complement one another in painting a picture of the dynamic social character of identities. Each of these traditions is instructive to later discussions of authenticity, multidimensionality, and mobility. They include symbolic interactionism, Goffman's dramaturgical sociology, Bourdieusian dispositional habit approaches to identity, modernity and postmodernity theoretical traditions, feminist standpoint theories and standpoint intersectional analysis, cognitive cultural sociology, and symbolic boundaries theories. I begin with symbolic interactionism, a theoretical perspective that develops directly from Mead's sociology of the self and that is widely viewed as the foundational theoretical perspective on the self and identity within sociology.

Symbolic Interactionism

As a foundational underpinning to sociological work in identity, symbolic interactionism has shaped several strands of recent identity research. Evolving from the social and philosophical pragmatism that took shape at the University of Chicago in the early twentieth century (the early Chicago School), symbolic interactionism emerged in the postwar era in response to the then dominant and mainstream structural functionalist paradigm that examined social phenomena primarily from a top-down macro focus (Carter and Fuller 2015). Structural functionalism stressed a rather singular and static view of social norms, institutional structures, and social relationships, while saying very little about the self and identity. As an alternative, symbolic interactionists stress that the meanings we associate with identities (our own and others), situations, and events emerge from our interactions with others in various contexts and communities.

Building on Mead's view of social activity among other influ-ences, symbolic interactionists bring the dynamics of human association to the fore of our concerns. They focus both on how people cooperate to come to a common understanding of their world (or fight over that understanding), and on how those with whom we interact (our individual and community affiliations) provide the foundations for our notions of self that, for inter-actionists, are deeply social and relational as well as projected through time. In short, meaning emerges from the real activity of human life and is maintained or changed via this dynamic activity as well. Herbert Blumer built further upon Mead's ideas, developing symbolic interactionism as both a theoretical and a methodological perspective for understanding the creative involve-ment of the self, the importance of context, and the complexities of social interaction in constructing identity. The methodological approach of symbolic interactionism emphasizes empirical inves-tigations of social life grounded in observable social interactions, and many of these investigations allow one to explore peer groups, reference groups, subcultures and other levels of group dynamics that deal with identity, in-group belonging and out-group exclu-sion, boundaries, codes, and symbols.

Symbolic interactionism's influence on sociology of identity research has been broad and varied. It has extended to social psychological perspectives on how individuals internalize roles and identities, as well to the more ethnographic traditions of research associated with the Chicago School, from which sym-bolic interactionism arose. These two traditions of research on identity both draw on symbolic interactionism's roots, but diverge from each other in ways that generate two different strands of research, catered to different scholarly audiences. The first tra-dition is heavily social psychological, focused on the individual and, methodologically, on experiment and hypothesis testing. It draws largely on Mead's interest in how the individual internal-izes the self and its roles from interactions with others. The second tradition is largely qualitative and ethnographic and builds on Blumer's methodological interest in observing meaning in social interactions. This latter tradition typically observes social actors in groups, as they interact in social settings.

Concern with the formation of the self in interpersonal inter-actions dates back as far as the works of Cooley (1964) at the beginning of the twentieth century and of Mead (Mead and Morris 1967) some thirty years later; their theories of internalized identities provided the insight that "we incorporate the social positions that we occupy into our cognitive image of ourselves as people" (see Owens, Robinson, and Smith-Lovin, 2010: 485). Mead and Cooley focused on how we internalize the way others see us. The self, in this view, is a social accomplishment produced through interactions with others. We learn to perceive ourselves through how others see us. A number of identity theories have originated from these insights.

One branch stemming from symbolic interactionist foundations consists of theories that are heavily focused on how identities and roles are attached to and internalized by individuals. Social psychological identity and social identity theorists in this tradition conduct social psychological experiments on how people behave in relation to their role identities. Burke and Stets (2009), for example, have developed a social psychological symbolic interactionist identity theory that looks at individuals' attempts to maintain and enhance self-esteem, to match their behaviors to standards relevant to their roles and identities, and to act in ways that keep perceptions of themselves in situated contexts, consistent with their identity and role commitments. Burke and Stets regard one's role (as reflected in what one does) as a basis for identity and examine the ways in which self-meaning attached to identity guides behavior in interaction.

As an example of their identity research, Stets and Burke (1996) analyzed how self-meanings of gender as a type of identity affected the negative and positive behavior of married couples whose task was to resolve marital disagreements. The two researchers hypothesized that those with a more masculine and more dominant control identity would be more likely to use negative behavior (e.g. complaints, put-downs, criticisms, defensive behavior, negative facial expressions, escalating negative affect) in their interactions, while those with more feminine and less dominant control identities would be more likely to use positive behavior. They tested these hypotheses using videotaped conversations from a representative sample of newly married couples and ran a factor analysis on coded responses. Stets and Burke found that wives rather than husbands employed more negative behavior in conversations but that, paradoxically, the results for being a woman were different from the results for being feminine, and the results for being a man were different from the results for being masculine. Men and women with more masculine gender identity standards were on average more likely to engage in negative behavior in order to bring their self-perceptions in tune with their identity standards, but women were on average more likely to engage in negative behaviors than men. In explaining these findings, Stets and Burke argue that women, as a social category, are culturally discredited in terms of competence and power and that this categorial discounting pushes them to counter discrediting disturbances to their self-concept through negatively coded behavior. This varies depending on the relationship; thus wives with more traditional husbands display more negative behaviors in interaction than do wives with less traditional husbands (Stets and Burke 1996: 213).

Stets and Burke regard identity as something performed at the individual level, in relation to identity standards and role expectations. They draw on symbolic interactionism's classical insights on role internalization, to analyze the social psychology of the individual. This kind of social psychological work is more psychological and laboratory-based than most of the work that falls under the umbrella of a symbolic interactionist sociology of identity, but this quantitative social psychological strand of research illustrates how widespread the use of symbolic interactionist elements is when applied to contemporary identity research.

Sheldon Stryker's structural symbolic interactionist identity theory is a similar social psychological and hypothesis-testing approach to the study of identity (Stryker 1980, 2008; Stryker and Burke 2000). Using Mead's conceptual frame to develop testable hypotheses, Stryker employs a role-theoretic sense of social structure to analyze identities as self-cognitions connected to roles and, through those roles, to positions in organized social relationships (see Stryker 2008: 20). Since in Mead's framework mind and self arise from accomplished, ongoing interactions where role taking plays a vital part in behavior, communication, and interaction, a role-theoretic sense of social structure illuminates the understanding of how symbolic interactionism plays out in everyday life. For Stryker (2008: 20), "social behavior is specified by taking 'role choice'—the opting by persons to meet expectations of one role rather than another—as that which [identity theory] seeks to explain."

Stryker develops structural symbolic interactionism as a revised Meadean approach that views social differentiation as a continuous process composed of organized systems of interactions and role relationships where these role relationships happen among complex constellations of "differentiated groups, communities, and institutions, cross-cut by a variety of demarcations based on class, age, gender, ethnicity, religion" and other variables (Stryker 2008: 19). In this view identities are self-cognitions connected to roles and, through roles, to positions in organized social relationships (Stryker 2008: 20). Identity attributes in this approach are organized into a salience hierarchy where different identities are more or less likely to be invoked in differing situations or relational and interactional contexts. And commitment, for Stryker, determines the source of immediate salience attached to identities. Stryker's structural symbolic interactionist identity theory recognizes identity attribute multidimensionality, seeing the self as multifaceted and comprised of "multiple identities arranged hierarchically in an identity salience structure" (Owens et al. 2010: 482).

Stryker specifically tests sets of hypotheses related to identity commitment, identity salience, and role performance. In particular, the theory addresses issues such as (1) behavioral consistency and inconsistency across different situations, (2) the degree to which people resist or accommodate change as they respond to changes in the structure of their interpersonal relations, (3) how people deal with conflicting role expectations, and (4) the allocation of resources for interpersonal interactions (see Stryker and Serpe 1982: 205).

As an example of Stryker's kind of theory testing, Stryker and Serpe (1982) tested role performance in the context of the religious role. They looked at the variables of religious commitment—as defined by relations to others, connected to the function or occupancy of a particular role, and measured by questions such as: "Think of those people most important to you. About how many would you lose contact with if you did not do the religious activities you do? And how many people do you know on a first name basis through your religious activities?"; they also considered factors such as salience of religious identity in relation to other identities and religious satisfaction. They found that commitment was predictive of identity salience and positively related to time spent in the role, performing that role.

Stryker's identity theory is concerned with the reciprocity of society and the self, but employs a view of society as a multidimensional mosaic of groups and institutions whose relationships run the full spectrum from cooperation to conflict (see Stryker and Serpe 1982). Stryker and Serpe share traditional symbolic interactionism's relatively narrow focus on roles and the self, but they develop a multidimensional view of the self as connected to a multifaceted social structure. As they explain, "if one adopts an image of society as complexly differentiated ... it follows from the premise that self reflects society that the self must also be complexly differentiated and organized" (Stryker and Serpe 1982: 206). Identity attributes, in this approach, are organized into a salience hierarchy where different identities are more or less likely to be invoked in differing situations or relational and interactional contexts. Stryker develops structural symbolic interactionism as a revised Meadean approach. Stryker is critical of Mead's view of society as differentiated only in a few ways and suggests that Mead's concept of the "generalized other" erases important distinctions between social structures that have significant variations, consequential for social interaction (Stryker 2008: 18). By introducing identity salience, Stryker's identity theory reminds us that identities are multifaceted. These saliences are also fluid and vary from context to context.

A second, more widespread tradition of symbolic interactionist theorizing is qualitative and ethnographic. Symbolic interactionists in this tradition employ qualitative methods such as participant observation, ethnography, and in-depth interviews in order to observe the symbolic worlds in which people live, operate, and interact. Drawing on Blumer's (1969: 2) three premises that (1) "Human beings act toward things on the basis of the meanings that the things have for them," (2) "The meaning of such things is derived from, or arises out of, the social interaction that one has with one's fellows," and (3) "These meanings are handled in, and modified through, an interpretive process used by the person in dealing with the things he encounters," they follow people's everyday activities in participant observation settings or through ethnographic depth interviews, in order to observe and understand people directly engaged in interaction and meaning making. Theorists in this tradition have broadened Mead's focus on the self and Mead and Blumer's emphasis on the standpoint of the individual actor, to include focusing on situations (e.g. Goffman 1961; Tavory 2016), groups (e.g. Fine 1979; 2012), places, and institutions. Gary Fine and Iddo Tavory (2019: 461–2) observe, for instance, that people are not in the world alone, and that it is through their groups and affiliations that they engage in sensemaking. Fine and Tavory (2019) highlight the utility of twenty-first-century symbolic interactionist perspectives for understanding identity, noting that Mead was not interested in situations or groups, but that contemporary interactionism takes the group seriously as an arena of commitment. They further note that contemporary symbolic interactionism has increasing theoretical and political interests in challenging and resisting oppression and privilege, a concern largely absent from early symbolic interactionism (Fine and Tavory 2019: 465).

Fine's (2012) group-based theoretical approach to ethnography, to which he refers as a *peopled ethnography*, represents the kind of methodological shift found in current qualitative symbolic interactionist approaches. Fine contrasts peopled ethnography, which is theoretical and generalizable in its focus, with personal ethnography, which involves thick description of a local, substantive site for the purpose of particularistic understandings rather than theoretical generalizability. Among the important elements of a symbolic interactionist peopled ethnography are (1) that it is theoretical and generalizable to conceptual questions that transcend the site, (2) that it builds on other ethnographic and research studies, and (3) that it examines interacting small groups in ongoing scenes where interaction is generally part of a continuous relationship (Fine 2012: 52–3). Fine's modern symbolic interactionist approach uses group interactions in scenes as the primary research site from which interactional-level data can be brought to bear on larger, macro-sociological concerns. Symbolic interactionism, in its modern iterations, shows a greater interest than its foundational beginnings in groups and situations and in applying insights from the study of group interactions to big issues such as social inequalities, cultural repertoires, social change, and the social reproduction of domination and privilege. These newer approaches to symbolic interactionism have become widely integrated into the mainstream of qualitative sociological research. As such, they often intersect with many of the other theoretical traditions mentioned in this chapter.

A movement from emphasis on the self to situations where social actors navigate their identities in interaction with groups and audiences has occurred within interactionist traditions in relation to Goffman's dramaturgical approach to observing social identities in varying peopled contexts.

Goffman's Dramaturgy: Identity as Strategic Performance

Sara, a 24-year-old heterosexual cisgender Korean American woman, wakes up in the suburbs on a Friday and stands in front of the mirror, contemplating what she'll wear to work today for her job at the insurance company. She wants to present herself as a professional person, so she plans to dress up. But it's also Friday, and she's noticed that her older co-workers, who have been in the job for a long time, dress more casually on Fridays. She notices that this is especially true among her older white male colleagues, who are able to exercise a degree of privilege, both from their dominant race and sex attributes and from the time they clocked up in the organization, to dress comfortably on casual Fridays and still be regarded as professional. Reasoning that she hasn't been in the job as long and that she has to do more to appear "professional," she opts for dressing only slightly more casually than she does on the other work days. After work she will change out of her professional outfit, into a dress and heels, to meet up in the city with her group, mostly white friends of the same age; and they will hit some Friday night clubs to dance, order a couple of carefully selected cocktails that convey sophistication, and perhaps engage in a few conversations with men whom she comes into contact with while caravanning in her same-sex group of friends. Later that weekend she'll make another trip into the city, to visit her grandparents, who immigrated to the United States from Korea. While visiting family, she will dress in Korean fashion, speak Korean with her grandparents, and accentuate the ethnic Korean parts of herself. Sara's presentation of self changes as she goes from work to the club scene and to her grandparents. Her performance of her identity and her appearance change and adapt with the context and with the audience she is performing for. She is strategically performing her identity as a resource of impression management. We all perform our identities strategically.

Erving Goffman's (1959) dramaturgical approach to identity draws attention to the strategic fluidity of identity presentation in everyday life. Goffman (1959, 1986) introduced and popularized the concept of social identity, demonstrating that identity is situated in social relations, interactions, and encounters. Goffman (1959) conducted fieldwork on the presentation of self among Shetland Islanders, analyzing how individuals play a role in order for observers to receive a favorable impression of who they are. His conclusions apply generally to impression management as a means by which people present and navigate their social selves across time and place. Goffman shifted the emphasis away from the internal features of self-identity and from the idea that we have an underlying "true self" that we carry from situation to situation, to demonstrate how elements of the situation and context themselves shape identity, cognition, and presentation. He draws us to the notion of a fluid and mobile social self that, like a chameleon, can change and adapt across different settings rather than remain fixed and never change its colors. Rather than a permanent set of fixed "true colors" tied to an inner core, identity is a mobile strategic resource, which changes as settings and audiences make different demands on one's identity. Goffman highlights the *strategic performance* of identities, establishing a tradition in sociological research that conceives of identity as performative (see also Butler 1990).

The idea of identity as a situated performance or as an interactional accomplishment draws from the tradition of Goffman as well as from Harold Garfinkel's (1967) ethnomethodology. Garfinkel advanced ethnomethodology as a perspective designed to analyze how the seemingly "objective" properties of social life become so through the situated conduct of societal members. He demonstrates that much of social life has a taken-for-granted character to it, because social structure is reproduced in subtle everyday practices that give human-created structures the appearance of objective realities. Identity is therefore an ongoing interactional accomplishment. Whereas Goffman views identity as consciously strategic, Garfinkel locates it more in the mundane, embodied features of everyday accountability, where one's status is always potentially open to question. Both theorists, while differing in their view of strategic interaction, point to the continuous movement of social identity in the navigations of everyday life.

A vibrant tradition in understanding gender, race, class, difference, and identity has developed from the roots of Goffman's and Garfinkel's interest in interaction and identity; this development includes West and Zimmerman's (1987) analysis of how we *do gender* as an everyday accomplishment that reproduces gender as a social structure, and West and Fenstermaker's (1995) illustration of how we *do difference* (specifically with respect to gender, class, and race) in our everyday interactions. Thus, for instance, individuals are always accountable for presenting identities and they present gender, class, and race through a wide range of mundane practices. Such works have shaped a growing interest in identity research that looks at how we "do intersectionality" or a multidimensional mix of attributes simultaneously. Later on we will look more closely at the ways in which people do multidimensional identities in their interactions with one another (see chapter 4).

Bourdieu's Habits and Dispositional Identities

Much of identity in daily life is not consciously calculated but rather practiced dispositionally, as automatic embodied habits (Bourdieu and Wacquant 2002; Bottero 2010: 3). Through experiences of social interaction in the form of repetition, imitation, and role-play, we informally acquire a set of dispositions and habits that guide our social instincts and give us a "feel for the game" (Bourdieu 1984; Swartz 2002: 63S). Bourdieu (1984) emphasizes habitus as the sum and essence of our ingrained habits, skills, and dispositions, a faculty that shapes how we carry ourselves and how we perceive and react to the world around us. Because these dispositions are acquired through our socialization and imitation of those around us, we tend to share similar dispositions with people who are like us in social class, education, profession, religion, ethnicity, and nationality. Bourdieu focuses heavily on dispositions rather than conscious reflection as the primary guiding force in social life. In this respect, his view of identity is quite different from Goffman's sense of the social actor as a performer, keenly aware of his or her audience and consciously manipulating the others' impressions of him or her in order to be seen in a favorable light.

A Bourdieusian approach suggests that identity is not a playful performance, easily manipulated, but a deeply etched set of unconscious investments that have been formed over time through socialization, experience, and repetition. Thus, in this view, gender identities for example are not surface-level performances of doing gender, but deeply rooted investments in practical, social relations, where embodied enactments of masculinity and femininity are reproduced in relatively automatic ways, often with no conscious intention of performing gender. Likewise, while social class strongly shapes our lives and we perform it every day, few people identify strongly and consciously with their own class, or mobilize explicitly as a social class. Instead we often perform our class identities repeatedly and unconsciously, in how we walk and talk, how we dress, what we consume, and what we do with our leisure time.

Bourdieu and Bourdieusian analysts of identity remind us of the importance of the tacit and taken-for-granted element of many identities and identity performances. While Bourdieu restricted his focus to dispositional identities, the distinction between these and more consciously mobilized identities is an important one to keep in mind (see Bottero 2010: 5). Social movement theorists, analysts of nationalism, and theorists studying the ways we do ethnicity, race, and gender have tended to focus on the most visibly, deliberatively conscious displays, but national identity, ethnic identity, race, and gender are also performed in subtle embodied habits. Situated in the routine embodied habits of everyday life, nationalism for example is performed not just in the high-intensity and conscious display of someone conspicuously waving a flag with fervent passion, but also in the barely noticed flag routinely flying from a public building (see Billig 1995: 8; Bottero 2010: 6). Likewise, social class is performed not just in the conspicuous display of a wealthy person ordering an extraordinarily expensive bottle of wine, but in the routine everyday practice of a lower-middle-class child boarding a relatively crowded school bus to attend a local public school.

The distinction between unconsciously dispositional and consciously mobilized identities is relevant to understanding the role of normative social power. As Bottero (2010: 7) notes, Bourdieu's dispositional view of identity is rarely used in accounts of racial identities where there are flourishing reflexive, mobilized forms of identity with great social and political significance. This is because analysis of racial identities largely focuses on members of minority groups who, by the nature of their social position, are unlikely to be afforded the luxury of remaining unreflective about race, and thus of being able to perform it without consideration or deliberation. Majoritarian racial identities—such as white identity in most of the United States—are quite easily performed, however, as tacit identities embedded in the unconscious practices of daily racialized living, with little sense that one is doing racial identity (Hagerman 2018).

Feminist Social Standpoint Theories and Intersectional Analyses

As our dispositions are acquired through daily interactions within our social networks and with institutions that categorize and treat us, in part, on the basis of our own categories, we share dispositions with others, who are similar to us on salient dimensions such as race, class, gender, sexuality, education and profession. This insight has been particularly applied to race, class, gender, and sexuality. Social standpoint theories, a line of theorizing that has emerged from feminist research traditions in the social sciences, have emphasized the importance of social location to identity. Social location refers to where a person's social characteristics and relative status within a social system place that person within a hierarchy of social value. Most notably, how does an individual's gender, race, or class shape his or her life experiences and worldview? Standpoint theorists have traditionally focused on marginalized, minority standpoints, which have been analytically ignored by social theorists who, unreflexively, assume that majoritarian standpoints are "neutral" and "objective" lenses from which one can interpret reality. Nancy Hartsock (1983), for example, argued for an understanding of society from a women's feminist standpoint, claiming that the structure of society is often more visible from the vantage point of the marginalized. Outlining gender as the central organizing feature of social life and as the central identity through which women are marginalized and men are privileged, feminist standpoint theorists explain both how gender is embedded in everyday life and how it shapes the conscious vantage point of women. Masculine men, having a privileged vantage point, can often take their positions for granted and regard them as objective. Standpoint theorists have taken an interest in politically salient collective identity attributes and on how these attributes shape self-identity. Drawing on Hughes's (1945) observations that some people have "master statuses" that inhibit their ability to be generic and unmarked social actors, standpoint theorists analyze the more salient dimensions of identity, which take on master status qualities. In this respect, standpoint theorists of the self and self-identity owe more to Hughes than to Mead.

While interactionists emphasize the social nature of identity by locating it within the social context, social standpoint theorists add to our understanding of the social nature of identity by introducing the relationship between social power and social location. If early symbolic interactionist theories focused on identity as the product of implicitly "generic" interpersonal social relations and micro-interactions, standpoint-based theorists view identities as socially structured, namely structured on the basis of the demographic categories people belong to and of how the relationship between those and other categories shape their experiences, their identifications, their vantage points, their worldviews, and their identities. We construct our social selves, in part, by navigating our constellation of salient collective identity attributes. These attributes are tied to various degrees of privilege and marginalization and to the politics of inclusion and exclusion.

Within more recent feminist scholarship there has been considerable interest in intersectionality and in analyzing how different social standpoints connected to marginalized race, class, ethnicity, gender, and sexuality categories intersect with and influence one another in the overall constitution of the self. Patricia Hill Collins (2019) identifies intersectionality as an inequality-based insight that recognizes that race, class, gender, sexuality, ethnicity, nation, ability, and age do not operate as exclusive domains, but are involved with one another in constructing phenomena, and that intersectionality as a knowledge project is attentive to power relations and social inequalities (see also Hill Collins and Bilge 2016). Standpoint and intersectionality theorists share with symbolic interactionists and dramaturgical theorists an interest in identity as a social feature and as a value partly produced in social interaction, but they add to analyzing identity a dimension that is more explicitly related to inequalities; and this dimension is often more subtle, or is absent in the earlier symbolic interactionist and dramaturgical theories of identity. That identities are intersectional, or multidimensional, is now widely understood across identity research; and the concept of intersectionality developed within black feminist traditions (see Crenshaw 1991) is now widely applied to interpreting identity construction. The idea of intersectionality points to the multidimensional character of identity and allows us to consider the complicated ways in which marginalized attributes interact with privileging attributes in how we present and construct ourselves and the groups we belong to. Multidimensionality is one of three centralizing analytic themes employed in this book to understand the social consequences of identity; and I will return in detail to multidimensionality and intersectionality in chapter 4.

Fluid, Fragmented, Flexible, and Depthless Identities: Modernity and Postmodernity Theories

While intersectionality theorists focus on the multidimensional interplay of intersecting identity attributes, postmodern theorists emphasize the multifaceted, fluid nature of our social relationships. The situational and relational elements of identity are especially highlighted in a globalizing world where technology, migration, and the pace and movement of social life leave open many possibilities for multiple relations and environments. The multiplicity of our involvements and their influence on the self are issues of concern for scholars interested in the relation between modern social life and the self. The social psychologist Kenneth Gergen (1991) discusses the frenetic state of the modern (or postmodern) self, where individuals are confronted with competing demands on their time and drawn in multiple directions. Modernity and postmodernity theorists of the self employ the language of multiplicity and fragmentation rather than the language of intersectionality and promote a different theoretical agenda from that of intersectionality theorists; but, while addressing very different theoretical topics, both groups deal with the multidimensional complexity of identity. Intersectionality theorists emphasize the integration of different attributes, while modernity and postmodernity theorists emphasize fragmentation and fluidity.

In her ethnographic analysis of identity in the age of the internet,

Sherry Turkle (1997) argues that identity is becoming decentered and multiple. People can join multiple online communities, adopt a different persona, and create several aliases without a requirement to reconcile these identities in a coherent or consistent unity (Turkle 1997; Davis 2011). Theorists concerned with postmodernity contend that the ability to rapidly switch identities and constantly take on new roles undermines the sense of a singular, coherent, authentic self. The self becomes entirely exterior and relationally oriented, in a highly fluid social environment; in fact it is almost entirely other-directed, with little opportunity to slow down and get anchored. The depth of a core self is replaced by multiple and rapidly changing surfaces (Davis 2011)—or so modernity and postmodernity theories argue.

Modernity and postmodernity perspectives emphasize the multiplicity of modern demands, the fragmented global reference groups and audiences we interact with, and the ways technological expansion speeds up the fluidity of relational identities. These perspectives draw attention not only to the increasing multidimensionality of modern identities, but to their mobility and fluidity. But, rather than see this fluidity as a challenge to self-identities, as these theorists often do, one can explore mobility and fluidity as dimensions of identity that allow for situated presentations of authenticity and for ways to organize multidimensional facets of the self across time and space and social networks.

Cultural Sociology: Culture and Cognition and Symbolic Moral Boundary Theories

Identity work is boundary work. People and institutions reinforce and maintain boundaries through interaction invested with cultural meanings. Culture and cognition and symbolic moral boundary approaches address the centrality of cultural meaning making that occurs through the categorization, perception, presentation, and expression of identities. One key perceptual element in the cultural meaning and interactional consequences of identities is the relationship between the socially and culturally *marked* and the socially and culturally *unmarked* (see Waugh 1982; Brekhus 1996, 2015; Zerubavel 2018). These terms, originally developed in linguistics to describe language contrasts in which one side is endowed with a mark, while the other is passively characterized by the absence of a specific mark (see Trubetzkoy and Jakobson 1975: 162), apply to social contrasts just as well (see Waugh 1982; Brekhus 1996, 1998). We observe the social world unevenly, noticing and stressing culturally marked elements as *socially specialized*, while largely ignoring culturally unmarked elements and taking them for granted, as *socially generic* (Brekhus 2015: 25; Zerubavel 2018: 2). The marked term signals a characteristic that remains unsignaled in the unmarked (see Waugh 1982: 301). For example, in most contexts transgender is marked, cisgender is unmarked; blind is marked, sighted is unmarked; foreigner is marked, native is unmarked; homeless is marked, domiciled is unmarked; polygamist is marked, monogamist is unmarked; fundamentalist is marked, moderate is unmarked; wheelchair user is marked, pedestrian is unmarked. In the marked–unmarked distinction the marked element is perceived as a more narrowly specified category, which coheres in a way in which the unmarked is assumed not to. Consequently, characteristics of a marked member are generalized to the marked category, while generalizations about the unmarked member are seen as either unique to the individual or generalizable as non-group-specific and applicable to everyone (Brekhus 1998: 36). The important contrast in the relationship is between the specialized category and the default "generic" category. Markedness is contextual. There are contexts where usual standards of markedness are reversed and what is marked in most other contexts is taken for granted. Where markedness is reversed from standard settings, generalizations about the contextually marked follow patterns similar to those found when the unmarked generalizes about the marked in other contexts. Thus gay patrons in a gay bar, for example, are likely to regard heterosexuals present in the bar as a category of people that are more coherent and easier to generalize about than the diverse mix of gay people present.

The power of the unmarked is that its implied universal representativeness normalizes and privileges the unmarked at the expense of the marked; but this privilege is often hidden (Brekhus 1998; Zerubavel 2018). Populations, individuals, and attributes not identified specifically by race, class, sex or gender, sexuality, region of the world, and age are more likely to be or belong to respectively white, middle-class, male, heterosexual, western, and non-elderly adults. These unmarked categories are often cognitively perceived as undifferentiated from the general standard, and thus come to serve as the default, but non-inclusive representatives of the universal. The most heavily marked categories, by contrast, are often cognitively perceived as "master statuses": statuses that not only differentiate the marked member from the general, but through their accentuated salience can often crowd out or wash over the social relevance of that member's less marked attributes.

The weight and salience that people attribute to various markers of identity and to various identities are heavily influenced by cultural and subcultural patterns of cognition and perception (Brekhus 2015). Theorists of culture and cognition emphasize the importance of intersubjectively shared patterns of cultural markedness and unmarkedness to the construction and maintenance of social categories and boundaries of marked exclusion and unmarked privilege.

Identification in the weaker sense and identity in the stronger sense are closely tied to cultural categorization. Categories are often first defined from the outside, but are accepted and repurposed by members of an identity category. The construction of identities is accomplished through interactional practices and through the boundary work of drawing lines of us–them, inclusion–exclusion. These lines are also symbolically reinforced through practices that establish the categories. Cultural sociologists emphasize the ways boundaries are shaped by the narratives and cultural repertoires (Swidler 2003) that people have access to and that are embedded in social and institutional environments rather than created by atomized individuals (Lamont and Molnár 2002: 171). Lamont and Molnár advance the need to understand identity beyond the realm of psychology; they tell us that we need to address "how conceptions of self-worth and group boundaries are shaped by institutionalized definitions of cultural membership—a topic rarely visited by social psychologists working on the self and identity." Brubaker and Copper (2000: 15) similarly indicate the importance of powerful, authoritative institutions such as the state and the legal system for creating formalized, codified, objectified systems of categorization that can be imposed on others with the weight of significant power. While the state, the legal system, the medical system, and the educational system are among the most powerful categorizers, they do not have a monopoly on the construction and diffusion of identities. Social movements and other, less for-malized categorizers may contest, challenge, revise, and refurbish official categorizations of identity.

Understanding collective identities as the product of boundary making requires a recognition of the importance of symbolic bound-ary making and marking. Identity categories are given some of their form and shape through mundane acts of performing taste, status, and lifestyle as if these were classificatory distinctions endowed with implicit moral weight. Pierre Bourdieu's (1984) concept of *symbolic distinction*—whereby one's category and status are performed and reproduced in acts of status differentiation in which people embody the *cultural capital* that marks their social position—is useful to the understanding of identity work. Performing distinction enacts identification and identity by demarcating boundaries that reflect a symbolically exclusive cultural membership. Cultural markers of class status can be used, for instance to symbolize and rationalize or naturalize social boundaries, and to reinforce their social weight. Bourdieu focused specifically on cultural capital and social position; but performing distinctions applies to multiple kinds of boundaries (Lamont 1992; Lamont and Molnár 2002). Lamont and Molnár (2002: 169) argue that symbolic boundaries exist at the intersub-jective level of socially shared definitions that are internalized, and that these symbolic boundaries lead to social boundaries that mani-fest themselves as groupings of individuals who practice inclusion and exclusion.

Whether we think of them as national boundaries, ethnic boundaries, religious boundaries, neighborhood boundaries, sub-cultural boundaries, or professional boundaries, an important part of collective identity construction is demarcating the boundaries between "us" and "them," between insiders and outsiders, between "natives" and "tourists" or "strangers" to a shared community. As suggested in social identity theory, "pressures to evaluate one's own group positively through in-group/out-group comparison lead social groups to differentiate themselves from each other" (Tajfel and Turner 1986: 16–17). This often produces a symbolic elevation of one's own group as having some desirable character-istics by comparison with others. Such in-group favoritism allows high-status groups to consolidate prestige and privilege. It allows lower-status groups to bond together in solidarity against discrim-ination, engage in collective agency, and make group demands.

Individuals and social groups engage in symbolic boundary maintenance and identity affirmation using cultural and subcultural patterns of markedness (accented marginality or accented extraordinariness) and unmarkedness (unaccented privilege) to inform the distinctions they make and the value they assign to those distinctions. Identity is often constructed by identifying who we are, by asserting who and what we are not. In the course of everyday life we often erect symbolic boundaries in our interactions that draw upon and reinforce more durable and institutionalized social boundaries or social differences (Pachucki, Pendergrass, and Lamont 2007). Cultural sociologists emphasize the ways in which we make distinctions, both narratively and in practice, in order to symbolically differentiate ourselves from others. In her analysis of "cultural omnivores" with cosmopolitan and worldly tastes, Bethany Bryson (1996) shows that omnivores define their own musical tastes in imprecise ways, stating that they like "all kinds of music" and reflecting an openness to diverse cultural experiences, while being quite specific about genres (heavy metal, rap, country, gospel, and other genres associated with lower-status, parochial "cultural univores") they do not listen to. The distinction between broadly undifferentiated, acceptable genres and very specific, symbolically "polluted" genres shows that omnivores define their tolerant identities by marking for exclusion genres that they associate with less cultured, more parochial people and taste categories. Cultural sociologists analyzing white working-class identities have illustrated how some working-class individuals create an affirming identity and exude a sense of dignity by symbolically differentiating themselves from others. Michèle Lamont (2000) shows that white working-class men differentiate themselves from black working-class men by emphasizing their "disciplined self" and discipline as a distinctive quality of self, while black working-class men differentiate themselves morally by emphasizing their "caring self." Symbolic differentiation also occurs in mundane practices, for example in the choice of clothing and appearance; we have seen in the introduction how working-class Mexican American teenagers and middle-class white teenagers in the same school chose lipstick and makeup colors that are intentionally symbolically distinct from each other. We will turn more to the symbolic elements of identity presentation in chapter 3, where I explore how collectives and individuals who establish their social identity within groups perform identity authenticity. One of the ways in which individuals can establish authenticity as members of a collective is by symbolically distancing themselves from less authentic others, impostors, or wannabes, and also from categories they are in opposition with. Emphasizing symbolic exclusion through taste and lifestyle choices establishes one's commitment to the in-group and its identity. Authenticity claims are also made by displaying, knowing, and embodying the "cultural capital" or "subcultural capital" associated with and expected of the group.

Varying Theoretical Traditions, Unifying Themes

The range of theoretical traditions concerned with the sociology of identities is broad, even dizzying. These traditions vary in their approaches and in their specific foci when it comes to identity. Symbolic interactionists' interests range from relatively narrow, foundational ones, for instance in analyzing how self-meaning attached to identity guides behavior in interaction, to more elaborate interests in how groups, in scenes, construct boundaries and identities. Dramaturgical theorists analyze the strategic uses of identity as a presentational resource across different settings. Bourdieusian theorists examine the habitual, taken-for-granted, unconscious dispositional aspects of doing identity. Intersectional standpoint theorists observe the ways in which multiple attributes work together in shaping identities, worldviews, and dimensions of oppression. Postmodern theorists highlight the fragmented, fluid, mobile nature of modern identities, in a world with ever wider and more far-reaching technologies and with increasingly dividing demands on selves. Cultural cognitive theorists emphasize the multidimensionality and culturally contextual impact of social categories, pointing to the combination of multidimensionality and mobility.

These varying approaches, while developing from different foundational roots and having different specific interests in identity, can inform one another and be brought together in scholarly conversation, so as to enhance our conceptual understanding of the sociology of identities. Much of this dialogue across traditions is already occurring, and can be further encouraged and illuminated by bringing this plurality of traditions together, around three current central themes in sociology of identity research. These themes are identity authenticity (the degree to which people try to authenticate personal selves or group belonging), identity multidimensionality (the ways in which people navigate the multiple intersecting elements that make up their self-identity or collective identity), and identity mobility (the strategies and currencies people use to navigate transitory and migratory shifts in their selves or collective identities).

Further Reading

Simmel, Georg. 1969 [1955]. *The Web of Group Affiliations*, translated by Kurt H. Wolff. Glencoe, IL: Free Press.

Among classical sociological theorists, Simmel is especially influential in thinking about role and social identity. His insights into "the web of group affiliations" provide an important foundation for understanding identity in the modern world.

Hughes, Everett C. 1945. "Dilemmas and Contradictions of Status." *American Journal of Sociology* 50(5): 353–9.

Hughes's short essay introduces the critical concept of master status, which is important for understanding totalizing identities. Hughes also introduces the idea of auxiliary characteristics associated with master statuses.

Stryker, Sheldon. 2008. "From Mead to a Structural Symbolic Interactionism and Beyond." *Annual Review of Sociology* 34(1): 15–31.

Stryker's structural symbolic interactionism revises Mead's approach to the self by placing greater emphasis on the differentiated roles and group commitments we have. Our identity attributes are organized into a salience hierarchy where different roles or identities are more likely to be invoked in different relational contexts. Stryker discusses this approach, what it draws from Mead and where it diverges, and suggests future directions for this approach.

Fine, Gary Alan, and Iddo Tavory. 2019. "Interactionism in the Twenty-First Century: A Letter on Being-in-a-Meaningful-World." *Symbolic Interaction* 42(3): 457–67.

Fine and Tavory provide a blueprint for how to approach interactionism today. Arguing that modern interactionism needs to be linked more closely to the sociology of culture, to group identity, and to oppression and privilege, they emphasize the significance of affordances, situational webs, group commitment, disruption, and embeddedness to illustrating the relationships between privilege and oppression.

Goffman, Erving. 1959. *The Presentation of Self in Everyday Life.* New York: Anchor.
Goffman's classic study of self-presentation is a foundational treatise on the dynamic uses of self-presentation as a resource for impression management. This approach to understanding the self as contextual and related to audiences shapes a significant body of sociological work in the sociology of identity.
Bourdieu, Pierre. 1984. *Distinction: A Social Critique of the Judgement of Taste.* Cambridge, MA: Harvard University Press.
Bourdieu's analysis of the habits, tastes, and aesthetic styles people develop and embody as a result of their socialization demonstrates how people reproduce social class through their embodied dispositions. This approach focuses on the ingrained but largely unconscious ways in which we reproduce class identities. The analytic implications of this framework can also be applied beyond class, to other dispositional identities.
Hill Collins, Patricia, and Sirma Bilge. 2016. *Intersectionality.* Cambridge: Polity.
Hill Collins and Bilge provide an overview of the concept of intersectionality, emphasizing the core ideas of the intersectional framework, how it relates to critical inquiry and praxis, and its implications for the study of identity.
Zerubavel, Eviatar. 2018. *Taken for Granted: The Remarkable Power of the Unremarkable.* Princeton, NJ: Princeton University Press.
Zerubavel takes the reader on a journey through the various ways in which we use language to mark some identity attributes as warranting special attention, and thus we tacitly construct normalcy in what remains unmentioned. This approach illustrates the culturally cognitive dimensions of perception and of producing and reproducing social privilege.
Lamont, Michèle, and Virág Molnár. 2002. "The Study of Boundaries across the Social Sciences." *Annual Review of Sociology* 28: 167–95.
Lamont and Molnár provide an analysis of research on

boundaries in the social sciences that is instructive for under-standing the critical role symbolic boundaries play in identity construction and in creating social boundaries that manifest themselves as groupings of individuals.

2

Beyond the Individual

Collective Identities

The classic identity question is "Who am I?' But equally important to identity are the questions "Who are we?" and "Who are they?" Identity is not lodged deep inside the individual. It is formed in the social world. Sociologists of identity have long recognized this in observing that people form their self-identities in relation to others (e.g. Mead and Morris 1967). But this is only half of the social story; identities are also social in the broader sense that social groups and collectives larger than the individual construct, form, and enact identities in relation to others. Identity is not just the individual formation of the "me" but the group formation of the "we."

An important idea here is the notion of *collective agency* (Cerulo 1997: 393)—the idea that entities can act collectively, as a social actor or agent. The perception of groups as active agents who make decisions and involve themselves in contemplating who they are and who they are not has been fueled by the rise of identity-based social and nationalist movements (Cerulo 1997: 386). Such movements are motivated by collective definitions and expressions of identity to advance political and cultural demands. Working within the social movements tradition, Polletta and Jasper (2001: 285) define collective identity as

> an individual's cognitive, moral, and emotional connection with a broader community, category, practice, or institution. It is a percep-
> tion of a shared status or relation, which may be imagined rather

than experienced directly, and it is distinct from personal identities, although it may form a part of a personal identity. A collective identity may have been first constructed by outsiders (for example, as in the case of "Hispanics" in [the United States]), who may still enforce it, but it depends on some acceptance by those to whom it is applied. Collective identities are expressed in cultural materials— names, narratives, symbols, verbal styles, rituals, clothing, and so on—but not all cultural materials express collective identities.

Polletta and Jasper's definition emphasizes important elements of cognitive, moral, and emotional connection, a sense of shared community and category membership, and practices or strategies of identity expression. Their idea of collective identity focuses on how the individual identifies with a collective; but one can also envision collectives themselves, and not just the individual's connection to a larger collective, as presenting an identity and exercising agency. Subcultures, professions, neighborhoods, and organizations are all social forms that can be seen as deploying and expressing collective identities. Collectives strategically deploy identity for multiple uses. Social movements deploy identity to advocate political and cultural change. Subcultures deploy identity to express belonging, rebellion, or style. Organizations such as businesses and universities deploy identity to attract customers. Neighborhoods deploy identity to police the boundaries of who and what is included and excluded.

The idea that collectives can be agents and possess and express identities may seem controversial. Identity is, after all, often seen as a coherent "core essence" that resides in individuals. How can collectives, composed of multiple people, have an identity? How can entities or groups with a diverse collection of individuals manifest a coherent, recognizable identity as a single agent? Since groups are composed of multiple actors, they can't literally perform acts as just one agent; but they can, at various times and to varying degrees, move together as a collective with similar passions, motivations, and cognitive worldviews. The ability of entities to move and act and to present a widely shared collective identity is, however, complicated by their composition. The fact that collectives are composed of multiple individual actors poses some unique problems for identity that individuals do not have. The plural nature of collectives means that their identities are often debated, contested, and disputed among members of the group. Groups and organizations may have a dominant image of who they are or whom they represent to others, an image shaped by the more powerful individual agents within the collective, but members within the group may challenge this and offer their own alternative visions. The plural nature of collectives also means that, even when members are grouped under a single categorial label, the parts of the group are more diverse than a unified categorization implies. This is an issue we will return to when we discuss racial and ethnic categories.

While collectives are not individuals, the processes of collective identity and self-identity share many things. Statements of who we are bear distinct similarities to statements of who I am. Just as the individual forms his or her identity in interaction with and in relation to other individuals, the collective forms its identity in interaction with and in relation to other collectives. Just as individual identities are formed through self-identification in response to categorization from others, group identities are constructed through group self-definitions in response to categorization from the outside. Just as individual identities are made coherent through the construction of internal homogeneity out of the diverse elements of the self, collective identities are made coherent through the construction of homogeneity out of the diverse elements of the group. Just as individuals strive for a kind of authenticity that stays true to the self, categorial groups strive for authenticity and category members strive for an authenticity that remains true to the group. Just as individuals balance multidimensional, intersecting attributes of the self to construct a coherent self, collectives balance the multidimensionality of their diverse membership to construct a coherent group. And just as individual identities are fluid, mobile, and context-dependent, collective identities also shift and change across settings and audiences.

Collective identities form along a variety of lines. Nations, ethnic and racial categories, subcultures, cities, neighborhoods, families, generations, professions, and organizations all form identities and are attributed identities by others. Across these various types, some common dimensions of differentiation are the criteria of membership, the manner in which membership is acquired, the signification and expression of membership, the nature of claims to authenticity, and the fluidity or stability of membership.

To begin our exploration of collective identities, we can take a large collective such as a nation.

Nations as Identity Communities

What does it mean to be a nation? National identity is the symbolic elaboration of an imagined community believed to have things in common and to be different from others (Spillman 1997: 2–3). The process of establishing the commonalities and the boundaries of a nation and of endowing them with meaning is complicated and multifaceted. Benedict Anderson (1983) defines nations as *imagined communities* whose constituents share a horizontal comradeship and a sense of common purpose as a collective entity with elements of similar experience and interest. Nations are "imagined," because members of the community have not experienced direct interactions with most other members. They have never met and likely will never meet. Nonetheless people will love and die for their national community, as well as hate and kill in its name. The personal and cultural feeling of belonging to a nation can be intense even as direct connections to other members of the community are limited or illusionary. Rogers Brubaker (1992) analyzes citizenship and national identity in France and Germany, showing that the political community of a nation is expected to be a cultural community with shared identity, mores, and a shared national character. Membership in a nation is "collectively self-defined, and the cohesive power derives from an 'us–them' distinction that stresses superiority over other groups" (Herb 1999: 16). Groups with collective identity create bounded communities of inclusion by building a set of valued attributes that members (us) share, while also tying themselves together through a politics of opposition and exclusion (them). The construction of a national identity expresses a sense of kinship based on some degree of overlapping histories, customs, and genealogies (Wiebe 2002: 5).

Anderson and Brubaker both explore how cultural (language) and social (economy, technology, and immigration) factors contribute to and affect national identity. Anderson illustrates, for example, how religious communities used to be a dominant source of influence; they shared sacred languages such as Latin, which was spread across different populations that spoke a variety of non-sacred languages. Print capitalism, Anderson argues, gave rise to new linguistic groupings of readers, and these groupings facilitated the formation of nation-states. The advent of the printing press spread books and, later, newspapers, creating texts of the form we know today; and these texts facilitated the normalization of written languages such as English, French, and Spanish. The readers of these texts became a linguisitically unified audience that spent time on the same things at the same time, thus forming a "community" with the experience of sharing the same news or information with others. Anderson demonstrates how large entities, be they religious groups, language communities, or nations, can come to see their identity as a collective when they are unified by some common experience, even if that experience is remote and indirect.

Brubaker's finding that the political community of a nation is expected to be a cultural community with a shared identity and a national character is well illustrated in the recent construction and celebration of Helsinki's ambitious Oodi library (see Dudley 2019). The library's opening in December 2018 marked the hundredth anniversary of Finnish independence. It is no ordinary library; and journalist David Dudley (2019) remarks that "in a country that boasts one of the world's highest literacy rates, the arrival of the new central library in Helsinki last year was a kind of moon-landing-like moment of national bonding . . . Designed by Finnish architecture firm ALA and dubbed Oodi ('ode' in Finnish) the three-level structure is a kind of spruce-clad monument to the principles of Nordic society-building." The library was intentionally built with a ground floor that is an extension of the public square outside, which in turn is directly across from and on the same level as the Finnish Parliament House; in this way it serves symbolically as a place of national citizenship that brings old and new residents together, in common purpose (Dudley 2019).

Placed in the heart of Finland's capital and near many of its political and cultural institutions, the library was built as a reminder of the 2016 Finnish Library Act's mandate that libraries promote equal opportunities to civilization and culture and to participation in lifelong learning, active citizenship, democracy, and freedom of expression. To implement these goals, the Act indicates that the baselines should be commonality, diversity, and multiculturalism (see Lindberg 2016). In line with the tensions of identity, it highlights the commonality of active citizenship and a shared "we," while also celebrating difference. Speaking of the library's national importance, Tommi Laitio, Helsinki's executive director for culture and leisure, opened his talk with an image of Finland's brutal 1918 Civil War, which killed more than 30,000 people; many of them perished in harsh prison camps (Dudley 2019). Laitio started by referring to Finland's troubled national identity, to contrast this negative and divided past with a more hopeful and unified present. By emphasizing Finland's marked past, he advanced a redemptive narrative of the country's present identity as a nation and a people that have overcome hardships by finding a shared purpose and a common society within diversity:

> This progress from one of the poorest countries of Europe to one of the most prosperous has not been an accident. It's based on this idea that when there are so few of us—only 5.5 million people—everyone has to live up to their full potential. Our society is fundamentally dependent on people being able to trust the kindness of strangers. (Quoted in Dudley 2019)

If we return to Anderson's (1983) idea that imagined communities come to recognize a shared identity even when they haven't interacted directly, we can see that regarding strangers as members of one's trusted community is a positive aspect of the horizontal comradeship that this kind of identity creates. The library, for Laitio, is an architectural monument to Finnish civic engagement and to Finland's modern emphasis on education, literacy, and active citizenship as shared values that constitute its national character. In a time when concerns over migration, disruptive technologies, and climate change have fueled right-wing populist movements around Europe, Laitio sees long-term thinking around "we" as a buffer against the short-term thinking of "I." As he explains, "when people are afraid, they focus on short-term selfish solutions. They also start looking for scapegoats" (quoted in Dudley 2019). The Oodi library and Finland's Library Act are particularly ambitious attempts to create spaces that bring the people of an imagined national community together, in a horizontal community. They are an example of what Shils (1988) refers to as a "cultural center," a structure of activities, roles, and persons distinguished by active attachment to a system of core values. These centers, made up of and devised by political and cultural elites, are oriented toward both the country's own cultural periphery and the cultural core of other societies. They are intent on socializing and mobilizing the rest of the country around a common purpose.

Governments and civic leaders often engage in active collective identity work in order to facilitate a "we" identity. They build monuments and sites of commemoration. They design flags and commission anthems. They create uniforms for their soldiers and police. They deliver speeches that articulate the message "this is who we are."

In analyzing the centennials and bicentennials of the United States and Australia, Lyn Spillman (1997) argues that commemorative celebrations are social looking glasses in which people see themselves collectively. Thus collective identities are reflective, much like the looking-glass self (Cooley 1964) of personal identity. Each commemoration asked: "Where do 'we' stand in the world?" and "What do 'we' share?"—reflecting how nations think about their identities in relation both to others and to their shared values and solidarity (Spillman 1997: 144). At their respective bicentennials, Australians were more concerned with the first of these questions, about Australia's standing and status in relation to its peers, while Americans were more concerned with the second question, about the integration of the diverse and divided people that comprise their nation. These differences were tied to different histories:

> By 1976, when Americans were quite secure at the core of the nation-state system, but facing new and highly conspicuous integration problems, they had little reason to place much weight on the theme of international recognition, or to elaborate the theme as the Australians would do twelve years later. For Australians, on the other hand, though they were now citizens of an independent nation-state and certainly drew stronger boundaries between themselves and powerful others than they had done in 1888, concern with the views of significant international others continued to charge symbols of Australian national identity with meaning. (Spillman 1997: 145)

Just as biographical experience shapes personal identity, a nation's historical experience (a kind of collective biography) shapes its identity. Caught in the midst of a civil rights movement and an age of divisive cultural conflicts but able to take its global power for granted, the United States emphasized the political values its contentious communities share. By contrast, Australia, less able to take a privileged status in the world for granted, focused particularly on its standing in the world (Spillman 1997). Australia's concern with its position vis-à-vis its peers shows that collectives, like individuals, construct their identities around their interactions with and status among others.

Collectives as large as nations contain a more diverse membership than a unified and coherent identity would suggest. The stories that elites and other members of a nation tell about the "national self" and the "nation's biography" highlight some elements of that nation's history and its values, while submerging others. Ethnic majorities within nations often symbolically exclude and erase minorities from the dominant national story. American history, for example, often begins with its white history, and not with the native populations that existed generations before the first white settlers. The native inhabitants are often relegated to America's "pre-history," but marking something as pre-history essentially deems it irrelevant for inclusion in the "real" history of the land that everyone takes for granted (Zerubavel 1997: 86–7). As marginalized populations challenge national stories that are too exclusive in advancing a one-sided, majoritarian-flavored history and identity, they stress the complex, multidimensional nature of national identities and create new narratives that incorporate multiple voices.

Steve Fenton (2011: 15) argues, however, that multicultural redrawings of the national story often treat inclusion or integration as a mainly symbolic issue and that, without focusing on the material issues of good schooling, secure employment, and safe neighborhoods, they fall short of the wider aspects of social integration applicable to the entire population. Fenton critiques the "culturizing" of the problem of social inclusion as primarily an issue of how to handle ethnic minorities. This approach still implicitly marks an ethnic minority as a special, stigmatized part of the nation's identity, something to be managed and absorbed into a generic whole.

Nations are just one type of collective entity that construct identities concerned with the boundaries of inclusion and exclusion, the manner in which membership is acquired and expressed, the nature of claims to authenticity of membership, and the fixedness or flexibility of membership. As Anderson demonstrated, religions for example served many of the unifying capacities that nations took over later on, after the advent of print capitalism. And, even today, religions, while perhaps in much greater competition with nations and other collectives for identity dominance, still remain as holders of potentially powerful collective identities. Like religions, racial and ethnic categorial identities, too, compete with nations as sources of collective identity. Indeed, while each type of collective is different, there are in fact analytic commonalities across how nations, religions, and members of racial and ethnic categories construct identity.

Ethnic and Racial Category Collective Identities

Brubaker, Loveman, and Stamatov (2004: 47–9) argue that the empirical domains of nationalism, race, and ethnicity have been treated as analytically separate and have developed through largely non-overlapping literatures that sprang from different political concerns, and that this has caused analysts to lose sight of the analytic similarities that cut across these domains. As they explain, "if nation, for example, is famously treated as an 'imagined community' or a 'conceived order' this is no less true of ethnicity or race" (Brubaker et al. 2004: 48). Brubaker (2002, 2006) cautions that ethnic and racial collectives are categories with the potential for group formation, not groups in and of themselves. People do things with categories, and this can mean excluding categorially distinguished outsiders from particular domains of activity, distributing scarce resources to categorially defined insiders, classifying oneself and others, and doing "being ethnic" (Brubaker 2002: 169). Brubaker argues that ethnicity, race, and nation are best thought of as practical categories, cognitive schemas, cultural idioms, and political projects rather than reified groups, and that we look at *groupness* as a contextually fluid variable rather than as a stable entity. Treating groupness as a fluctuating process rather than regarding groups as fixed and given allows us to find variation between moments of high cohesion and intensely felt collective solidarity and periods when group-making efforts of ethnopolitical entrepreneurs fail to crystallize effectively into a sense of group solidarity (Brubaker 2002: 167). Brubaker distinguishes between *ethnopolitical entrepreneurs*, specialists of ethnicity committed to the strategic uses of group identity to mobilize and energize, and *ethnic non-specialists*, who can be motivated to intense groupness but often also do being ethnic—and do it in subtle and muted ways, without commitment to groupness. The notion of "groupness" as an abstract quality, rather than "group" as a concrete entity, and the concept of identity entrepreneurs who try to motivate group identities can both be applied to other collective identities beyond the ethnopolitical arena. Ethnopolitical entrepreneurs work to form collective solidarities and senses of belonging similar to the kinds of belonging that elites and leaders of nations (we might call these nationalism entrepreneurs) work to construct when trying to instill national group solidarity in imagined communities.

Ethnic and racial categories are other- and self-ascribed entities that are based on cultural classifications of ethnicity and race. These collective entities are defined as categories, and their prospective members often accept and demonstrate fitness for membership. The Norwegian anthropologist Frederik Barth argues that the experience of belonging in an ethnic group "implies a claim to be judged, and to judge oneself, by those standards that are relevant to that identity" (Barth 1969: 14). Members develop a sense of the standards one needs in order to be a "member in good standing," who demonstrates an appropriate level of authenticity and commitment to belonging to the category. As ethnicity is an organizing feature of social life, shared membership of an ethnic group can acquire a kind of master status where it is assumed that other common values and interests will follow. Barth (1969: 15) further adds:

> The identification of another person as a fellow member of an ethnic group implies a sharing of criteria for evaluation and judgement. It thus entails the assumption that the two are fundamentally "playing the same game," and this means that there is between them a potential for diversification and expansion of their social relationship to cover eventually all different sectors and domains of activity. On the other hand, a dichotomization of others as strangers, as members of another ethnic group, implies the recognition of limitations on shared understandings, differences in criteria for judgement

of value and performance, and a restriction of interaction to sectors of assumed common understanding and mutual interest.

In Barth's conception, for people, a sense of shared ethnicity in a relationship allows for other sectors, domains, and ways of organizing social life to follow. By contrast, the sense that one is of another category implies that the intersections of shared understandings and mutual interest contract rather than expand. A society may be fundamentally dependent on the trust of strangers, but the ethnic or categorial other is to be trusted in a more delimited range of spheres than is the ethnic or categorial insider. One of the alchemies of imagined communities is to allow "community members" to see a categorial insider who is technically a stranger as a non-stranger, someone who can be trusted and assumed to have enough in common with you to be recognized and safely included in all spheres.

Ethnic and racial groups are not as clearly bounded by land as nations. In consequence, the imaginary communities they form are more geographically fluid, but this does not necessarily reduce the members' sense of belonging to a collective "we." In her study of Mexican migrants in the United States, linguist Anna De Fina (2003) analyzed the relationship between individual and collective identity in the narratives of their personal experiences told by migrants in Langley Park, Maryland. Focusing on these narrators' choice of a pronoun, De Fina observed that Mexican migrants frequently told stories that were cast in the *nosotros* ("we") form; and they often did so in response to questions about their individual experiences. Mexican immigrants often presented their experiences not as unique, but as general and transferable to the similar experiences of other members of their ethnic community. This was further evident in how they often shifted focus from themselves as the center of a narrative to other characters in the story. As the interviewer, De Fina (2003: 70) often asked singular, individual *tu* (you) questions about autobiographical experiences, while the interviewees often switched to *nosotros* forms without explaining the new referents. They narrated their individual experiences as part of a larger collective such as their ethnicity, their community, or their family and relatives. At one level, Mexican migrants saw ethnic identity as a central component of their self-identities, negotiating it at the local level as a facet of the self. But they also articulated values, beliefs, and experiences they possessed in common with a larger community, a broader sense of belonging, and a collective sense of agency. Focusing on the distinction between stories of personal experience and chronicles of how they crossed the border, De Fina demonstrates that, in the latter, migrants used "we" language to suggest that agency emerged from the group rather than from the individual. In some instances, the use of the choral "we" occurred even when the speaker was an individual. When discussing the act of migration itself, they preferred pronominal language that downplayed the agency of an individual narrator while emphasizing collective identity and agency. Mexican immigrants used linguistic strategies that highlighted the centrality of the collectivity by comparison to the role of the individual, and in important aspects of their lives. As an ethnic category facing the hardships of a dangerous migration and of discrimination, Mexican immigrants developed a strong sense of community, group identity, and collective agency. The idea that the group itself is an actor, and that this actor sometimes takes center stage over the individual, goes a long way to show that identity is very much a social phenomenon. Identity is heavily influenced by situational circumstance. In the face of experiencing shared exclusion, members of oppressed categories are likely to give collective voice to the social groups to which they belong.

In a similar example of how a collective ethnic identity is constructed within the context of shared discrimination and injustice, Prins, van Steklenburg, Polletta, and Klandermans (2013) employ a narrative approach to understanding identity negotiation among second-generation Moroccan Dutch young adults, who are both an ethnic and a religious (Muslim) minority in the Netherlands. These second-generation ethnic immigrants, like De Fina's Mexican immigrant interviewees, often used pronouns that were revealing of a sense of collectively shared experiences. When discussing prejudice, for example, one interviewee explains: "when you're waiting for the tram or the bus and there's an old lady and she immediately grabs her bag. I absolutely hate that. That is a prejudice that everybody [Moroccan Dutch] here has experienced." He is using the pronoun "you" to suggest that his experience does not feel like an individual, isolated act but as a general one, shared with all members of his ethnic group.

Moroccan Dutch immigrants co-constructed a common collective narrative about their position in Dutch society that emphasized injustice and discrimination as features of life in this society, features that they experienced as a community. Moroccan Dutch identity was "defined through a collective narrative dominated by experiences of discrimination and injustice" (Prins et al. 2013: 95). Prins and co-authors demonstrate, however, that these narratives were sometimes complicated by "second stories" wherein a specific narrator would reassemble elements of the main collective story to emphasize individual components that complicated the generic narrative of a uniformly disadvantaged minority identity. These collective identities were relatively stable and enduring, but also fluid, in that they were subject to narrative revisions. While the fluidity of collective identities is something that will be examined in greater detail in chapter 5, a more immediate focus here is that the stories articulating a disadvantaged minority identity predominated in all the focus groups that Prins and colleagues interviewed. This demonstrates the significant strength of a unifying collective narrative that solidified a strong sense of group identity among second-generation Moroccan Dutch immigrants.

Racial identity, like ethnic identity, is another widely studied form of collective identity. Social movements around racial identities have often emphasized the need to see a racial category as a unified collective agent that operates for the purpose of social change. Often described as forms of "strategic essentialism," racial identity-based social movements project a common group identity with a sense of solidarity and agency.

With reference to black racial identity in the United States, Tommie Shelby (2002) distinguishes between thin and thick conceptions. In a thin conception, "black" is a socially imposed category of difference that is based on certain visible physical characteristics and on having biological ancestors who fit a qualifying profile. For those who meet the membership criterion, one is black as a matter of ascription and cannot escape membership (Shelby 2002: 239–40). A thick conception requires commitment to the social category and a more demanding set of criteria for who qualifies as authentically "black." This is often tied to a cultural conception of blackness that brings in an entire set of values, beliefs, practices, and behaviors that have come to be associated with "auxiliary characteristics" of blackness. Black identity in this conception is not just a thin identification associated with physical characteristics but a more intense and deeper connection with a seemingly coherent, tightly bounded category with a history and common interests of its own. Shelby argues that conceptions of ethnic and cultural versions of thick black identity as a basis for making social change claims require black individuals to identify with "black culture" and to view thick cultural and ethnic "blackness" as constitutive, at least partly, of who they are. Black people, he argues, must "actively *perform* their blackness" for others to see (Shelby 2002: 246). In contesting this model of strategic essentialism, Shelby argues that people can engage in social action and foster mutual trust of one another without requiring an expression of affiliation with other members through the display of an authentic black ethnic or cultural identity. The intense issues around performing identities as a signifier of commitment to the collective and as a measure of authenticity are significant ones, and they have to be examined both as to the nature of these claims to authenticity and membership and as to the uses of identity in collective social movements.

Social Movements as Collective Expressions of Group Agency and Identity

Given that many collective identity assertions are bolstered by people in categories that experience discrimination, social movements that respond to discrimination and symbolic exclusion are an important source of collective identity. Social movements develop a sense of collective agency as a group (Cerulo 1997: 393). They acquire collective definitions, symbols, cognitive frames, and claims to group power. Social movement identities are formed when people see themselves as part of a collective force, explicitly committed to social change (Jasper 1997: 86). Social movements may act in the name of a collective identity such as that of African Americans, gays and lesbians, or women, but a movement identity is distinct from a collective identity based simply on structural location alone (Jasper 1997: 86). Structural location, by itself, may lead only to the kinds of thin conceptions of identity that Shelby (2002) identified in his analysis of black identities; it lacks both the thick commitment and the collective agency of a social movement.

Taylor and Whittier (1999: 174) argue, similarly, that movement identities are not automatic with respect to structural position, but actively produced: "collective political actors do not exist de facto by virtue of individuals sharing a common structural location; they are created in the course of social movement activity. To understand any politicized identity community, it is necessary to analyze the social and political struggle that created the identity." Much of this struggle centers around how the group's interests conflict with the interests of the group's adversaries, who are often more powerfully connected to positions of dominance or to the dominant culture. Jasper (1997) argues that movement identities can be further broken down into organizational identity (the movement's organizational dimension), tactical identity (a movement wing's association with specific styles of tactics, e.g. radical vanguard), and activist identity (the movement's association with the broader subcultural aspects of being activist).

Before the mid-1980s, the social movement literature focused primarily on social movements as carriers of meanings and ideas that grew more or less automatically from structural arrangement, unanticipated events, or existing ideologies (Benford and Snow 2000: 613). Since then, social movement scholars interested in identity and meaning (e.g. Snow and Benford 1988) have viewed social movement actors as signifying agents, actively engaged in framing meaning for themselves and for antagonists, observers, and bystanders. In other words, such actors are invested in "the politics of signification" (Benford and Snow 2000: 613). Social movement scholars borrow from Goffman's (1974) concept of frame to use the term "framing" (Gamson et al. 1982; Snow et al. 1986; Snow and Benford 1988) to conceptualize the work that social movements do to signify. Social movements construct shared meanings or collective action frames to define what is going on, what should be going on, and who is involved, to motivate social action. Extending from Goffman's framing to Goffman's impression management, social movement scholars have become interested in the role of strategic identity. Goffman focused on the strategic presentation and impression management of identity in individuals. These same conceptual insights apply to collectives that also deploy identity as a strategic resource, shift and alter their identity tactics and presentations for different audiences, and engage in impression management.

In contrast to theories focused on ideology or resource mobilization, identity politics understandings of social movements focus on the ways collective identities, themselves, have increasingly become a significant basis for political action. As Cerulo (1997: 393) argues, "when moved by identity, collectives take on distinct properties." Sociologists developed an interest in social movements as identity communities, when identity-based movements (civil rights, women's rights, gay rights) emerged that advocated recognition of and respect for the cultural differences that derive from distinct group identities (Bernstein 2005: 49–50). Anspach (1979) first introduced the concept of *identity politics* to refer to the political activism of people with disabilities—an activism designed to change self- and societal conceptions of such people (see Bernstein 2005: 47). New social movement (NSM) theorists have adopted identity politics as a concept with broad applicability to the entire array of movements that have developed to demand social and cultural changes in the status treatment of marginalized groups. These new social movements, centered as they are on identity politics, advocate for specific changes in public policy and in cultural practices related to identity, status, lifestyle, and culture.

NSM theorists differentiate new, identity-based movements from more traditional social movements that focus instrumentally on economic and class-based demands. Scholars of NSMs observed that participation in gay rights, feminism, nuclear energy, war and peace, and other movements could not be predicted by class location (Polletta and Jasper 2001: 286) and that motivations did not seem to be focused on instrumental goals. Implicit in the distinction between these new, identity-based movements and established instrumental movements, Bernstein (2005: 49) argues, is an underlying neo-Marxist assumption in the latter that class inequality and economic oppression are the real sources of abusive power and exploitation, and thus the primary targets for meaningful social change. This kind of assumption is especially pronounced among some of the more vocal academic critics of identity politics, who see identity politics as cultural rather than structural, and therefore trivial when it comes to addressing the structural conditions of inequality (e.g. Kauffman 1990; Gitlin 1996; Spragens 1999). It is true, as Jasper (1997) has argued, that more of the NSMs, which he calls post-citizenship movements, have participants who already enjoy most or all of the normal rights of citizenship, including being able to legally mobilize and pressure decision makers (see also Polletta and Jasper 2001: 287), but this does not necessarily mean that such formations of shared identity are inherently less real than formations that are based on class—and not on cultural values or other status distinctions. Conflicts over identity politics, over how to deploy identity, and over the nature and authenticity of identity claims are significant, and the implication that class-based identity movements and claims are more "real" and "authentic" than other identity-based claims is, itself, an interesting social standpoint assumption. That analysts, united in a disciplinary perspective that regards class as primordial in relation to other identities, privilege it as a structurally more "real" basis for interests and social movements, does not negate the empirically observable moral and mobilizing significance of non-class-based collective identities in social movements.

The emergence of social movements committed to identity politics points to the considerable importance of collective identities. Identity politics movements develop a sense of collective agency that recognizes the group itself as an active agent (Cerulo 1997: 393–4). Perceiving the group as an actor affords it motives, emotions, and an identity that can be shaped and reshaped in power struggles, symbolic and instrumental battles, and social interaction. Much as an individual strives for authenticity, movements strive for the authenticity of their values and of their presentations of identity to others. In the context of social movements, collective identity examines how individuals combine a sense of who they are with a definition, shared by co-participants in the movement, that this is who "we" are (Gamson 1992: 55). Amy Binder (1999: 224) argues that "one of the primary means for creating collective identity is to cultivate for the group a firm sense of who one's enemies are; that is, who sits on the other side of the boundary marking 'us.'" "Who we are" requires, in social movements, an understanding of what positions members of the movement are expected to put on the agenda and what positions are excluded; and, in identity-based movements, an understanding of what types of members are directly included and which members fall outside the criteria for full, unqualified membership.

Organizational Identities

Many of the practices that go into nation-building and national identity construction also occur in smaller collectives. These smaller entities have more capacity for members to meet a higher percentage of other members, but they can still be imagined communities, in that members are unlikely to come into direct contact with all other members. Organizations, like nations, express their own identities. Just like nations, elites and leaders of organizations will attempt to shape cohesion within diversity by emphasizing a fundamental "we"-ness. And, as with nations, this cohesiveness is often a majoritarian claim within a more complex collective environment.

A university, for example, as an organization with a community and a history, constructs a collective identity. Like nations, it has its own monuments and sites of historical commemoration, its own anthems (the school alma mater), its school colors, and, if it hosts a sports team, its own mascot. Much like leaders of nations, university leaders attempt to balance the identity themes of commonality and difference within their multifaceted constituencies. And, as with nations, the collective identity of universities is sometimes contested, especially by those who see themselves excluded from majoritarian stories about the university. Just as national identity disputes often occur over who is and who is not included in the unified vision of what the nation is, so too do disputes within universities arise around the symbolic politics of inclusion and exclusion.

Armstrong and Hamilton (2015) show how the institutional priorities of a large public flagship state university present the school's identity and social atmosphere as a place where students can get a valuable social experience and meet like-minded friends. It is a familiar situation at many flagship public universities in the United States. Universities showcase their social environments by presenting to their students state-of-the-art recreation centers, athletic stadiums, luxury residence halls, and fraternity and sorority houses. These become important sites of collective identification with the university community, but they are also sites that support a particular kind of college experience, one that favors privileged majoritarian interests at the expense of others. Armstrong and

Hamilton refer to the dominant pathway that infrastructure such as the Greek fraternity and sorority system and big-time college athletics support as the *party pathway*. This pathway has come to characterize the dominant campus culture of most state public universities. Of the pathways Armstrong and Hamilton identify (party, mobility, and professional), the party pathway is the one embarked upon by the largest number of students. Universities increasingly present their organizational cultural identities to undergraduates, on the default assumption that students are likely to integrate into the majoritarian social culture and get interested in homecoming activities (which are dominated by fraternity and sorority involvement), large sporting events that bring the community together in a stadium, and other collective acts of identifying with the university as a community. These forms of integration are both collectively celebrated and symbolically exclusive, represent- ing majoritarian interests rather than inclusivity.

Armstrong and Hamilton show that the costs of emphasizing the university's social party pathway are to squeeze out infrastructure for an alternative, a *mobility pathway*. The party pathway, they show, benefits upper-middle-class and wealthy students with social and cultural capital who benefit from meeting friends and getting, without much rigorous work, a degree that they can none- theless translate into post-college success, thanks to their cultural capital and social class connections. But rural, working-class, and first-generation college students who lack the connections and social and cultural capital of their wealthier peers are largely excluded from the benefits of this pathway. Such students would benefit from more infrastructure for the mobility pathway, which is focused on academic support, financial aid, and the provision of rigor, more educationally nurturing skills, and a specifically academic focus.

The party pathway versus mobility pathway tension that Armstrong and Hamilton identify is about institutional resources and infrastructure, but it is also about the dominant student cul- ture and identity on campus. Organizations develop collective identities for what they are and for those who constitute the "we" of their communities and constituencies. Recent social movements on university campuses have often challenged majoritarian senses of "we," which exclude full representation of the multifaceted constituencies that make up the university. Challenges of this sort can take the form of symbolic acts such as dismantling majoritarian symbols of collective identity that include some at the expense of others. Black anti-racist students and their allies at Princeton, for example, organized a campaign to remove Woodrow Wilson's name from the Princeton School of Public and International Affairs, demanding that "Wilson's name no longer serve as a symbol of their school's collective identity" (Cairns 2017: 104). They argued that keeping Wilson's name in that position was a tacit acceptance of the fact that exclusions were built into membership; thus campus citizenship was rooted in an identity based on oppressive entitlement, which ignored and erased black members of the community (Cairns 2017: 104). Organizations such as nations and other bodies with collective identities present images, narratives, and symbols of those identities that express "who we are" and that are open to various levels of groupness, as members share and contest understandings and negotiate representations of collective identity.

City and Neighborhood Identities

A 2011 Super Bowl commercial for the luxury Chrysler 200 begins with a gruff masculine voiceover: "I got a question for you. What does this city [Detroit] know about luxury? What does a town that's been to hell and back know about the finer things in life?" Images of manufacturing plants, steel, and murals with brawny men working in them glide across the screen. The masculine voice continues:

> Well I'll tell ya. More than most. You see, it's the hottest fires that make the hardest steel. Add hard work and conviction and the know-how that runs generations deep in every last one of us. That's who we are. That's our story. Now its probably not the one you've been reading in the papers—the one being written by folks who have never been here and don't know what we're capable of.

Images of people flash across the scene: a multiracial group of men in American football sweatshirts jogging next to snow, an Arab American woman figure-skating, an African American man in uniform acting as a hotel valet parker, a white police officer directing traffic, and an African American man in a suit and hat walking along the sidewalk. The narration continues: "Because when it comes to luxury, it's as much about where it's from as who it's for. Now we're from America. But this isn't New York City or the Windy City or Sin City. And we're certainly no one's Emerald City." Detroit-born white hip-hop artist Eminem steps out of a luxury car. A sign saying "Keep Detroit Beautiful" rolls across the scene. Eminem walks into a church, stands in front of a singing African American choir, stares at the screen, points and assertively says: "This is the Motor City and this is what we do." The ad ends with white lettering on a black screen: "The Chrysler 200 has arrived. Imported from Detroit."

The narrative and images of this commercial—one of the most talked about in the history of the Super Bowl—play heavily on Detroit's identity as the gritty, tough Motor City; the intention is to market a luxury vehicle made in Detroit as authentic. While Chrysler was ultimately using Detroit's image to sell a product, the vividness with which it could capture Detroit as a place with a distinctive identity is noteworthy. Identity is something found not just in individuals but also in collective forms such as neighborhoods, cities, and regions. While the individual says "I am," the collective says "we are." As reflected in the commercial's statements—"That's who we are. That's our story" and "This is the Motor City and this is what we do"—claims around the identity of collective forms are plural claims to a shared "we" rather than singular claims to an unshared "I." If individual identity is often thought of as a core essence that makes the individual unique, collective claims balance asserting a unique identity for the collective with showing the common glue that binds people within that collective.

Similarities with individual identity stories are still evident in the stories of collective and place identity that we tell. Much as we use personal biographical narratives to construct our self-identities, the ad narrates Detroit as a place with a set of life experiences that shape who and what Detroit is. Like many of its workers who have fallen on hard times, Detroit itself has "been to hell and back." Knocked down by the loss of manufacturing jobs and beaten up upon by columnists in other cities who "have never been here and don't know what we're capable of," Detroit has nevertheless dusted itself off, got back up on its feet, and found redemption and rebirth (an identity story that Detroit leaders like to tell). The narrative of Detroit's repaired identity is not unlike narratives of personal redemption and identity restoration, in which an individual discusses rebirth from hardship, loss, sin, or addiction. The commercial also illustrates how identity is defined not only by who we are, but by who we are not. In this case Detroit, through the narrator's masculine voice, proclaims its proud pariah status as "no one's Emerald City" and defines itself against the more revered and widely respected cities of distant New York and nearby Chicago and the glitzier "sin city" of Las Vegas. Masculine, hard-working, racially mixed, and American, Detroit is represented as multifaceted and authentic. A final narrative twist, "imported from Detroit," plays on the city's marked status, to imply that Detroit may seem different and exotic, even foreign, to people from more privileged parts of the country, while at the same time staking a claim to the authenticity of Detroit's "American-made" style and taking a thinly veiled jab at actual foreign imports.

Detroit has a gendered, classed, and raced identity, shaped by its history, its economy, and the stories we tell about it. Just like individual identities, Detroit's identity is an ongoing, complex, and fluid project. It has changed over time. Known at various times in the 1940s as the "arsenal of democracy" for its role in assisting the production of jeeps, tanks, and bombers by rapidly transforming its auto economy, and as the "Motor City" for its central role in the automotive industry, Detroit has also been negatively marked, as the ultimate symbol of urban decay. This latter construction of Detroit, as a ghetto in decline, is one in which its identity is strongly coded as dangerous, poor, and black. It is this stigmatizing identity that the Chrysler commercial challenges; the ad's narrative of redemption parallels the city's own narrative, as leaders work to reinvent Detroit through the repurposing of old factory buildings for music scenes, artists' lofts, and urban nightlife and to rebrand the city's racial identity through an emphasis on multiethnic cosmopolitanism in public spaces (even if private space remains heavily segregated). The reinvention of Rustbelt cities through the development of downtown districts and waterfronts with shopping districts, riverboat casinos, sports stadiums, and aquariums designed to attract suburbanites, inviting them to commute to the city for leisure, and through the addition of artists' lofts and arts and theater venues designed to make urban "creative class" cosmopolitanites resettle, are growing trends (see Sugrue 2005: xxiii–xxiv) that are shifting the working-class, masculine, manufacturing identities of these cities. The racial, class, and gender identities of cities are shaped, of course, by the practices of people who live in them, especially of those people who have the power to zone the space and make decisions that affect employment, migration, and housing.

City planners and marketing consultants often take the lead in attempting to brand the identity of cities, with the intent of persuading people to try them on and see if they like them. A bit like how we market our personal identities on a dating app, these brandings are often strategic *impression management* (Goffman 1959) presentations of place identity that reveal the place's more favorable attributes and conceal its more stigmatizing ones. These branding efforts illustrate how we conceive of places as possessing their own distinct identities.

The self-narration projects of cities, advanced by community leaders, wrestle with the same issues that individuals grapple with in narrating their personal identities. How, for instance, do I convey a portrait of myself as unique, so as to appear interesting, but not so distinctive that I would be ostracized as abnormal, dangerous, undesirable, or deviant? Along these lines, city officials strive for their cities to be known as adventurous rather than dangerous, multicultural and cosmopolitan rather than racial and racially divided, creative and quirky rather than deviant.

The construction of mostly (but not exclusively) white college towns in the United States as something just a little bit different and interesting is one manifestation of how some cities attempt to balance the line between comfortable, unmarked normalcy and interesting distinctiveness. The city of Fargo, North Dakota, for example, brands itself as "north of normal," a clever slogan that plays on its geography in the northern part of the United States and capitalizes on the positive cultural association with the North as situated up on the map and hierarchically above other directions. This branding constructs Fargo as a little better, a creative oasis, a bit different from its bland, normal surroundings. At the same time north of normal also conveys a sense that normal is still at least on the same map, close at hand, a friendly neighbor to the south. Indeed, as in the case of cities that attempt to attract suburbanites to their artistic districts, the branding invites "normal" people to commute a little to the north and activate their more adventurous and esoteric sides by giving Fargo a go. As in Garrison Keillor's depiction of the fictional Minnesota town of Lake Wobegon, in the same part of the country, as a place where all the children are "above average," "north of normal" emphasizes difference in moderation. "North of normal" is less extreme than "abnormal." Likewise, above average is not an exceptional or an unusually deviant outlier, but rather somewhat better, yet still in the same neighborhood, an unmarked, unthreatening averageness. North of normal is cosmopolitan, multiethnic, artsy, creative, and free-spirited. The images in the marketing video of north of normal convey a vibrant community with creative people; the social class presentations appear to be largely middle and upper middle class. Like many college towns, Fargo is more educated and economically better off than its neighbors. Its social class position as a city among its surroundings is not wealthy and extraordinary, but above normal. For an Upper Midwestern college town that is largely white, middle class, politically moderate, and tolerant to accepting, but does not wildly embrace difference, north of normal is just right: it is a slogan that resonates with the moderate openness and above-averageness of this city, registering its measured difference from an underlying bedrock of unmarked Midwestern normalcy that it sits upon. Just as individuals navigate the balance between the exclusivity of distinctiveness and the privileged inclusivity of normalcy, so cities, too, through their representative voices, negotiate the complexity of their multifaceted identities by navigating between the strategic advantages of difference and of sameness.

While city officials and corporations with large advertising budgets have more power to shape the public faces of their cities, city identities are, of course, contested and debated across different constituencies and in different spaces of the city. The Chrysler ad "imported from Detroit" and Fargo's "north of normal" campaigns are not universally shared or undisputed claims to the authentic identities of Detroit and Fargo, but they are illustrative examples of some of the processes that social actors can use to assign identities to entities greater than individuals. The process of attributing identity to a city shares many things in common with processes of self-identity and self-identification. And as with self-identification, cities and neighborhoods define themselves against other cities and neighborhoods, much like individuals construct self-identity, in large part, by defining who they are not. Detroit is not New York City. Fargo is not normal, nor is it south of normal. Also, like individual identities, cities and neighborhoods can be seen as having identities that are largely fixed and immutable or ones that are contingent and fluid. Frederick Wherry (2011: 8) discusses, for instance, how neighborhoods in Philadelphia that are perceived as dangerous or disorganized can be regarded either as inherently "bad," "culturally deficient," "antagonistic" toward civil society, and unworthy of external interventions or publicly supported improvements or as contingent and relative spaces whose current dangers can be annulled through public art, community gatherings, improved intergroup relations, and other interventions. The former descriptions characterize an identity "bad" to its core and a place that should be geographically quarantined and avoided, while the latter depict a redeemable place, whose currently troubled or dangerous identity is subject to revision. Neighborhoods themselves, through their community leaders, understand this and attempt to contrast themselves with others, strategically addressing the mutability of their negative attributes and emphasizing positive aspects that could wash over them.

The idea that a collective entity such as a city can possess an identity may trouble those who regard identity as something essential that resides deep inside the individual. Yet, while identities can be felt deeply inside, as part of one's personal core, they are socially and culturally formed. Sociologists of identity have long recognized this feature when observing that we form our self-identities in relation to others; but identities are also social in a broader sense. The social world not only shapes us to construct and narrate self-identities, it also shapes us to construct identities in collective forms. The range of collective forms that identities take is broad and expansive and includes such entities as nations, cities, neighborhoods, social movements, subcultures, families, generations, occupations, and organizations. The "who we are" stories of collectives share significant elements with the "who I am" stories of individuals. Ultimately, no matter what collective identity form we look at, one of its key elements will be that it is engaged in the boundary and classification work of defining its own membership and of requiring members to authenticate it by demonstrating commitment to the collective and its interests. Moreover, like individuals, collectives, too, can have race, class, age, gender, and sexual identities.

Race, Class, Age, Gender, and Sexual Identities of Collective Forms such as Neighborhoods, Professions, and Industries

Just as identity itself is not limited to selves, neither are specific identity attributes such as race, class, age, gender and sexuality. Neighborhoods, places, organizations, industries, and other social forms are often ascribed—and develop—distinctive racial, class, ethnic, gender, age, and sexual identities. In large cities one can walk through the Jewish neighborhood, the Koreatown, the Hispanic barrio, the gay neighborhood (gayborhood), the Italian neighborhood, and the black neighborhood. In these neighborhoods and ethnic districts it is not just that the residents have ethnic, racial, or "ethnically gay" or Jewish identities; these are identities of the neighborhoods themselves. In the United States—where hypodescent ancestry rules mean that an individual's marked racial attribute as black holds more social weight in defining his or her racial identity than his or her unmarked whiteness, so that someone one-quarter black and three-quarter white is black—a kind of parallel logic seems to apply, whereby blackness weighs heavier than whiteness in the identities of racially mixed neighborhoods. There it is not unusual for white residents in a city to define neighborhoods that are 40% to 50% African American in their area as "black neighborhoods," and *tipping point* models (Schelling 1971) of white flight suggest that white residents will begin to move out of neighborhoods that are perceived as becoming "mixed" or "black" when relatively low thresholds of residents, around 13%, are black. The racial identity of neighborhoods, like that of individuals, is more heavily defined by racially marked members and attributes.

Racial and ethnic enclave neighborhoods engage in identity presentations that "do difference" and emphasize commitment to an identity. Just as individuals use identity as a strategic resource to emphasize and highlight some facets of their selves and to downplay others, neighborhoods and other collectives deploy identity strategically. An individual can display ethnic pride and amplify his or her identity as an ethnic lifestyler, or can do so strategically, on some occasions, while downplaying it on others as an ethnic commuter, or can manifest a permanent low-density ethnic identity, as an ethnic integrator. Neighborhoods deploy identities in similar ways. Wherry (2011: 8) notes that, as postindustrial cities have worked to replace the loss of manufacturing jobs with cultural tourism, leisure cosmopolitanism, urban nightlife, arts, and cultural industries, they have taken a growing interest in the impression management of the city's ethnic neighborhoods. This impression management focuses heavily on representing diverse neighborhoods as having each its own ethnic flavor or being ethnically authentic. Focusing on a Latino neighborhood's construction of "Latin soul" and "Latin flavor," Wherry demonstrates some of the performances of the neighborhood's ethnic identity, both among its residents and among outsiders in search of an authentic ethnic experience. Riding on a trolley tour through the barrio, Wherry (2011: 28) listens as the tour guide points to the first of many Puerto Rican flags that hang outside a warehouse and announces: "as you can see, we are entering the Puerto Rican neighborhood." Wherry indicates that there is no actual need to proclaim that the flags mark the end of the "non-ethnic" Center City and the start of a new "ethnic" neighborhood, defined by its ethnicity, but that the statement serves as a reminder that the trolley is moving into a site of celebrated identity difference. A significant dilemma that neighborhood branders face is balancing ethnic markedness in a way that makes the neighborhood a site where identity difference is celebrated as "cultural" rather than feared as "dangerous" or "deviant."

In the construction of neighborhood identity, various kinds of practices of symbolic distinction can perform the work of reinforcing one's status within a socially valued collective. In her ethnography of a white working-class neighborhood in Chicago, Maria Kefalas (2003) shows how residents use their taste and lifestyle practices to symbolically defend the neighborhood's identity and its boundaries from what they see as dangerous incursions of disorder in the form of crack, crime, graffiti, gangs, and single-parent welfare families, which threaten them as public housing residents are relocated in the area. Showing how ecological factors and physical features of the landscape are deployed to mark identity, Kefalas observes that residents cultivate their gardens, keep their lawns tightly manicured, keep their homes clean, maintain and guard their property, and take great care of their American cars—all this by way of drawing a line and establishing a distinction of taste and identity between the normative and orderly decency of their garden community of bungalows and the chaotic forces of "the ghetto." Kefalas demonstrates the kind of symbolic boundary work that goes into maintaining a sense of "American respectability" and safe order in the face of threatening disorder. As in the identity work that Philadelphia barrio neighborhoods engage in when they attempt to combat disorder with public art (see Wherry 2011: 8), here too the deployment of markers in the landscape further solidifies a sense of order, safety, and community as characteristics of the neighborhood and its people. These symbolic boundary distinctions designed to strengthen the inner sense of community and identity are also exclusionary practices, which define what and who is "out of place." Keeping weeds out of the garden and taming the nature of disorderly lawns is metaphorically related to maintaining a sense of human order, so that desirable members of a community are encouraged to flourish, while "invasive problems" that threaten the sense of order are unwelcome—symbolically, and perhaps materially as well.

Just as some neighborhoods have an ethnic identity, other neighborhoods have a distinctive sexual identity. Much as the presence of Puerto Rican flags indicates a transition into a neighborhood with a marked ethnic identity, as one reaches the Castro district in San Francisco, one will see rainbow flags that signify the district's gay identity adorning the neighborhood. Gay enclaves such as this one, or the Village in New York, or West Hollywood in Los Angeles arose as sites of concentrated gay identity during the post-World War II era. These sites, known as "gay ghettos" (Levine 1979), gay enclaves, or "gayborhoods" (Ghaziani 2015), nurtured quasi-ethnic gay communities with an entire host of dedicated institutions such as gay bars, gay bookstores, gay-owned businesses, gay bathhouses, gay gyms, and the like. In an era when most gay men were "in the closet," hiding their sexual identity, gayborhoods expressed an openly gay collective identity. Demonstrating the true power of the collective, these neighborhoods were often more visibly and openly gay as whole communities than as sums of their individual parts. Gay enclaves created a critical mass of institutions and support that manifested a strong identity of place; for this reason they were a mecca for people who wanted to live as gay people or to visit the enclave and do gay identity while in its space. These gayborhoods, with their visible clustering of gay residents, gay tourists, and gay businesses and with quasi-ethnic gay symbols such as the rainbow flag, are residential sites that express an identity in a concentrated, vibrant, visible form. As gay identity becomes less stigmatized and less marginalized, these intense sites of gay identity are still recognized as entities whose attributes are important, but they are becoming less entirely gay and more multidimensional; they have acquired a mixed sense of cosmopolitan gay-friendly identity (see Ghaziani 2015). Neighborhoods navigate their identities and experience identity shifts and transitions over time like other collectives and individuals. The relative weight of various attributes that define a place, an organization, or an individual is fluid across time, as different histories and events shape and reshape identity. Greater acceptance of gay identity, and its decline in markedness, have prompted many gay people to move out of the gay havens of urban areas into more unmarked social and residential spaces. The lower markedness of gayness has also led to a corresponding increase in non-gay migrants to traditionally gay neighborhoods.

Just as neighborhoods can have ethnic, racial, or sexual identities, professions, too, have identities that are raced, classed, gendered, or sexualized. Industries such as mining, logging, and construction are masculine in the collective identities they give rise to, even as they have a range of more masculine to more feminine individuals working in them. In his ethnographic study of firefighters, Matthew Desmond (2007) reveals the gendered, classed, and regioned identity of wildfire fighters. Individuals in the industry heavily police gender and co-construct a very masculine collective persona. In the performance of their occupation, firefighters constantly do gender as a performance of collective country masculinity. Desmond explains that "certain bodies, deemed precious, are protected, while others, deemed expendable, protect"; this principle generates the complex ways in which people who enter firefighting, who are (relatively) socially expendable because of their low social class position, navigate their self and occupational identities. Firefighters do or perform risk in order to protect others and tie this to their masculinity and to their image as protectors—fearless strong men, antithetical to weak and feminine people (including weak and feminine men). Theirs is an intersectional "country" masculinity that is not only gendered, but also regional. In their view, the distinction between rugged "country boys" and sheltered, sissy "city boys" is an important identity distinction, which extends to their doing hard and risky outdoor work. City boys are indoor types who lack the ability to survive on their own in the dangerous wild, while they, the firefighters, have the skills and the *country competence* (a form of rural and masculine cultural capital) to thrive in the wilderness (see Desmond 2007: 42–6). In defining their profession and themselves as male risk-takers with rustic or "country" competence, firefighters also construct the other as a paradigm of feminine incompetence and equate the urban and suburban class with effeminacy. One of Desmond's firefighters explains:

> There's nothing wrong with being a city boy. Like *you*, there's nothing wrong with being in the city. You're a pretty boy, you can't help it. You get hit on by guys all the time, you just like that. You like the attention. *That's* what a city boy is. They just love the attention of being hit on by other guys, I mean, regardless if they are homosexual or not you know, I know most of them aren't, but they just like the attention, and that's a city boy.

This is meant to suggest that city, effeminacy, and homosexuality are all intersectional, intertwined, and very different from the world of the country boy, who is masculine and unquestioningly heterosexual and displays a rustic know how.

The symbolic work of representing membership in one's nation, profession, social movement, or neighborhood consists in recognizing shared membership and in engaging in rituals of membership affirmation. We will turn some more to the symbolic elements of identity presentation in chapter 3, where I explore how collectives and individuals establishing social identity within groups perform identity authenticity. One of the ways in which individuals can establish their authenticity as members of a collective is by symbolically distancing themselves from impostors or wannabes and from categories they oppose. Emphasizing symbolic exclusion through taste and lifestyle choices establishes one's commitment to the in-group and to its identity. Authenticity claims are also made by displaying, knowing, and embodying the cultural or subcultural capital associated with the group and expected of its members.

In closing this chapter, I should note what collective identity is not. Polletta and Jasper (2001: 298) express the distinction between collective identities and personal identity by stating that "collective identities are in constant interplay with personal identities but they are not the aggregate of individuals' identities. If collective identity describes what makes people occupying a category similar, personal identity is the bundle of traits that we believe make us unique." Individuals may incorporate the characteristics of collectives they belong to and define themselves through attributes such as nation, race, ethnicity, religion, and region, and these can become part of their multidimensional individual identities.

Further Reading

Anderson, Benedict. 1983. *Imagined Communities: Reflections on the Origin and Spread of Nationalism.* London: Verso.
Anderson defines nations as imagined communities that have a sense of common purpose even as most members will never have direct interactions with most other members. Anderson's is foundational work in the field of social construction of collective identities.

Spillman, Lyn. 1997. *Nation and Commemoration: Creating National Identities in the United States and Australia.* Cambridge: Cambridge University Press.
Spillman analyzes the role of commemoration in constructing collective national identities by showing how the bicentennials of the United States and Australia reflected the nation's concerns at the time, for example internal integration of a diverse and divided people (a special concern in the United States) and status positioning in the world vis-à-vis one's peers (a main concern in Australia).

Brubaker, Rogers. 2002. "Ethnicity without Groups." *European Journal of Sociology / Archives Européennes de Sociologie* 43(2): 163–89.

Brubaker, Rogers. 2006. *Ethnicity without Groups.* Cambridge, MA: Harvard University Press.
Brubaker's book is a provocative challenge to the idea that

groups exist. He argues that, rather than seeing ethnicity in terms of ethnic groups, we should focus on the categorial and cognitive processes that construct ethnicity. He proposes the idea of a more flexible groupness rather than one of enduring coherent groups. Brubaker provides orienting warnings for the sociologists engaged in the study of collective identities.

De Fina, Anna. 2003. *Identity in Narrative: A Study of Immigrant Discourse*. Amsterdam: John Benjamins.

Linguist De Fina analyzes the links between narrative discourse and identity construction, showing how people use narrative styles and ways of telling stories to negotiate membership categories and construct collective identities. Her case study involves the narrative constructions of Mexican immigrants to the United States.

Armstrong, Elizabeth A., and Laura T. Hamilton. 2015. *Paying for the Party: How College Maintains Inequality*. Cambridge, MA: Harvard University Press.

Armstrong and Hamilton illustrate how organizations such as universities develop public identities and market themselves to students. They study ethnographically a large public flagship university and demonstrate that this institution caters for upper-class and upper-middle-class students by supporting a social "party pathway," which comes at the expense of less wealthy, economic mobility-oriented students. Armstrong and Hamilton reveal how the university's dominant campus culture and identity have costs for less privileged members of the student body.

Wherry, Frederick. 2011. *The Philadelphia Barrio: The Arts, Branding, and Neighborhood Transformation*. Chicago, IL: University of Chicago Press.

Wherry analyzes neighborhood identities, demonstrating how a so-called bad neighborhood engages in community branding in order to change its reputation and identity through strategies of integrating arts and local businesses with ideas of ethnic authenticity.

Kefalas, Maria. 2003. *Working-Class Heroes: Protecting Home, Community, and Nation in a Chicago Neighborhood*. Berkeley: University of California Press.

Kefalas illustrates how residents of a white working-class neighborhood cultivate their gardens, manicure their lawns, and maintain their properties to symbolically confront "disorder" and to maintain a sense of neighborhood exclusivity vis-à-vis black public housing residents.

Desmond, Matthew. 2007. *On the Fireline: Living and Dying with Wildland Firefighters*. Chicago, IL: University of Chicago Press. In his ethnography of wildland firefighters, Desmond analyzes how firefighters construct their identities, occupational as well as individual. Central to their construction of identity are expressions of "country competence" (a form of rural and masculine cultural capital) and an intersectional "rugged masculinity."

3

Performing Authenticity

Negotiating the Symbolic Politics of Inclusion and Exclusion

Collectives, through their members, and individuals strive for authenticity. People in contemporary societies regard some things as real and authentic and other things as mere pretense and inauthentic. As individuals and as members of groups, subcultures, and organizations, we want to appear authentic to ourselves and to others. Authenticity is an important part of social life, but authenticity is a social accomplishment, an interactional performance, or a narrative claim—not a core essence. Performing authenticity gives us meaning and a sense of belonging. We show up at a rock concert wearing band t-shirts and engaging in talk about the show that will signify that we are authentic fans of the genre or of the group. We search out a city we are visiting for an authentic Mexican restaurant. Finding what is called in the United States a small "hole in the wall" sort of place (that is, a modest, out of the way restaurant) and hearing the kitchen staff speaking Spanish to one another, we feel good about our selection. We tell others that we are free-thinking, complicated individuals who don't conform to fads and fashions and don't go along with the crowd. We contemplate whether we are being true to ourselves, whether we are living an authentic life with meaning. We wonder whether our ever-increasing interactions with people outside "real," physical space, in the virtual world, are genuine and whether our online communities are authentic forms of community or thin facades. We work to prove ourselves in communities to which we belong and to show that we are committed to our nation, our religion, our city, our organization, or our social movement. All these are examples of the ways we negotiate and perform identity authenticity. What does it mean to be real rather than fake? How do we demonstrate authenticity to ourselves and to others? Defining and performing identity authenticity are activities that help us to construct boundaries of belonging and not belonging and to situate ourselves within the symbolic politics of inclusion and exclusion.

Self-Authenticity versus Collective Authenticity

One dilemma in unpacking identity authenticity is that claims to an authentic "personal self" that stays true to one's "core self" and claims to authentic group membership that stay true to a collective identity are at odds with each other. Establishing an authentic personal identity involves emphasizing our unique biographies, personalities, interests, and sets of skills and experiences, as they define us and differentiate us from others. We are interesting and authentic because we are unique and multidimensional. By contrast, performing group authenticity, that is, the kind of authenticity that expresses a group's identity, requires us to emphasize characteristics that are not idiosyncratic, but rather common to the collective group or to the crowd as a whole. Rather than differentiate ourselves, we perform core markers that highlight our membership in a collective made up of similar and like-minded people. Differentiation is still performed in opposition to the styles of other groups, of course, but the performance of group authenticity is also a presentation of significant within-group sameness. The analytic distinction between self-authenticity and collective authenticity is important because people can simultaneously attempt to perform both, even as the ultimate goals (uniqueness and commonality) appear to be in direct opposition to each other.

Traditionally, given the origins of identity research in psychology, concern with authenticity has focused on self-authenticity. The foundational roots of this concern go back to philosophers such as Jean-Jacques Rousseau, who regarded authenticity as an essence of human beings that had been stripped away by living in societies, and Friedrich Nietzsche, who, one century later, saw the self as threatened by social forces. Other philosophers, for example Martin Heidegger and Jean-Paul Sartre, posited that the authentic self could be rooted in a personal responsibility meaningfully engaged with the world (see Williams 2019: 607). From these philosophical ideas an interest in self-authenticity and individual autonomy has sprung up in the social sciences; and it continues. Freudian theorists, for example, have been concerned with the repression of hidden parts of the self and the presentation of what they saw as inauthentic selves, or the potential for false self-behavior in close relationships (see Chodrow 1978; Harter 1997: 86–7). In his analysis of "false" and "true selves," David Riesman (1950) distinguishes between inner-directed people, who are self-determining and therefore "more authentic" or true to themselves, and outer-directed individuals, who conform to social demands and are therefore "less authentic" or true to themselves. Gergen (1991) has focused on the challenges to the "authentic self" that the increasing demands and commitments of modern society place on individuals, suggesting that the self is diluting or dissolving under the strains of postmodernity.

Embedded in the logic of Riesman's and Gergen's approaches is the idea that inner-directed people—who can fight off the pressures of powerful social forces and maintain a personal boundary that protects them from the incursions of a social world that places external demands on the self—are more authentic than those who lose themselves as they make efforts to conform to the world around them. This view assumes that personal identity, and therefore personal authenticity, are tied to an individual core. To be true to oneself is to be true to one's private, non-social core. Yet, if the self is socially formed through our biography, our experiences, and our interactions in the social world, there is no reason to assume that its authenticity is somehow located internally, away from the world that shapes it. The strategic deployment of the self in the face of shifting social roles and cultural contexts, an idea drawn from Goffman's (1959) dramaturgical view of the self, suggests that conceptualizations of authenticity can be tied to the social context, and not to an individual core. Mark Snyder (1987), in analyzing psychological self-monitoring, defines self-regulating behavior as effective role adaptation to context rather than inauthentic self-deception. Being conscious of one's surroundings and presenting to others one's identity with a sense of awareness of what is expected of one's role in the given setting, while a performance of self, need not be seen as a false performance, but rather as a contextual self-performance that is true to one's role and place in the moment. And, while the contextual self may seem incomplete because it omits some attributes from its immediate performance, this incompleteness does not necessarily create a false self so much as a partial self, which is true to what is most salient in a person's immediate setting and relationships.

Ralph Turner (1976) distinguishes between people recognizing their real selves in feelings and actions of an institutional nature and people recognizing their true selves in the experience of impulse. Those who anchor the self in institutions see the true self as aligned with institutional values of ambition, morality, and altruism and realize their real self through achievement. Those who anchor the self in impulse see institutions as artificial constraints to the true self, and find theirs through a process of discovery. Under the institutional view, the real self is responsibly integrated with institutional demands and is in control of the person's behavior, while under the impulse view the real self is revealed when the person's inhibitions are lowered or abandoned. For "institutionals," hypocrisy means failing to live up to one's desirable moral standards and ambitions; for "impulsives," hypocrisy means putting on a fake, socially acceptable front rather than expressing one's true desires (Turner 1976: 994). These contrasting views on the relationship between institutions and the "true self" reveal the socially constructed nature of self-authenticity. They are tied to completely different visions of authenticity. The controversy as to whether the self is more authentic when it is shaped by institutions or when it is freed from the constraints of social control is reflected in discrepancies between authenticity accounts from individuals, and even in differing conceptions of authenticity among analysts.

Concerns with identity authenticity have gradually come to place greater focus on the contextual nature of selves and a stronger emphasis on group authenticity. Establishing authenticity vis-à-vis an identity (whether a self-identity or a group identity) is a complex and potentially contested process, and one based on deploying the right symbolic and interactional resources to authenticate an identity claim.

Authentication works in multiple directions. Consider, for instance, the typology in Brekhus (2003) of three different ways in which gay men in the New York–New Jersey metropolitan area authenticate their gay identities. Some men "lifestyle": that is, they practice this social identity as a "master status" that strongly shapes all aspects of their life. The gay lifestyler lives in a gay-specific enclave, works in a gay job, immerses himself in mostly gay social networks, and polices his identity performances and those of others so as to ensure that everyone is acting "authentically gay." For the lifestyler, authenticity is about being a central part of the gay community, demonstrating pride and commitment to it, and organizing one's life so as to contribute to and be an integral part of that community. Navigating an authenticity related to a lifestyler's identity requires consistently demonstrating the auxiliary characteristics expected of full members of the community. *Auxiliary characteristics* are the expected behavioral and presentational traits associated with a status role or identity (see Hughes 1945; Brekhus 2003: 1–2). The policing and the performance of auxiliary characteristics are means by which we show commitment to the requirements expected of and associated with a given identity. Other men, in Brekhus (2003), "commute" to their gay identity. They live in the suburbs and travel to the city to enact these identities. Whereas "gay identity" is basically a master status for gay lifestylers, for gay commuters it is something that they do. It is an identity that is amplified and actively performed in gay-friendly settings, but is not visually deployed in less gay-friendly environs. The gay commuter is a social chameleon, who code-switches his auxiliary characteristics to match the setting. For the commuter, authenticity is contextual and performed with an eye to one's audience and to the particular identity and status that one is accountable for in the given moment. Still other gay men "integrate" their gay identity into a larger, multifaceted self. They perform a self-identity wherein their gay identity is just one in a larger combination of attributes that help to flavor the larger whole. For the integrator, authenticity comes in the performance of a self shaped by the many attributes or flavors that comprise who one is, rather than in the focused performance of the auxiliary characteristics of any single attribute of a collective identity.

A typology of identity strategies centered around lifestyling, commuting to, or integrating a collective identity attribute such as gayness or being gay demonstrates that authenticity can mean very different things to different people. For someone lifestyling a collective identity attribute, authenticity is about establishing one's belonging to or one's central place in the group. For someone commuting to a collective identity attribute, authenticity is about establishing one's ability to belong and to get along in social environments. For someone integrating a collective identity attribute, authenticity is crafted by balancing one's multiple collective identity commitments into an individual self that is multifaceted and unique. Noteworthy is that each identity strategy type—lifestylers, commuters, and integrators—claims authenticity for its style of identity presentation. Each person in one of these categories says, in effect, "this is who I really am, and therefore it's fine." Consequently, authenticity claims act as *vocabularies of motive* (Mills 1940) that justify people's identity strategy and persuade others of the acceptability and desirability of their actions. For lifestylers, claims to authenticity as members of a group involve: (1) a strong commitment to that group's identity, as evidenced by time (duration) and intensity (density) of performing it; (2) the accentuation of auxiliary characteristics associated with doing the identity in a pure, untainted, undiluted form; and (3) demonstrating that the identity is something meaningful that comes from the core of who one is and is not a mere affectation or a cynical performance. Authenticating these three elements is a cultural negotiation where the battle is fought on two fronts: duration and density. Duration refers to the period over which one does the identity, both in terms of performing it consistently in the present and in terms of claiming it as an enduring part of who one is over the entire life course. Density refers to how thickly, intensely, or convincingly one enacts the identity and performs it as a display of one's true colors and commitments. Commuters share the lifestylers' commitment to performing an identity with intensity, but do not see the fixedness of high duration as more authentic than the flexible ability to adapt to different environments. Integrators share the lifestylers' interest in duration but reject the high-density presentation of auxiliary characteristics, seeing authenticity instead in the ability to present group identity not as a master status or greedy identity that crowds out competing identities, but as one part of an integrated whole.

While authenticity can mean very different things to different people, its multiple meanings are often missed in everyday life battles over it. People are likely to see their own meanings and performances of authenticity as appropriate or "real" measures and to judge the competing performances of others by their own standards. Oppositional subcultures and minority groups, as socially marked populations, are often perceptually defined by their most visible members. Lifestyler vocabularies of motive associated with high-duration and high-density performance are therefore prominent in debates over authenticity and inauthenticity.

Individuals perform authenticity through the expression and accentuation of auxiliary characteristics associated with an identity and by emphasizing forms of *subcultural capital* (Thornton 1996) valued within the group. On the basis of his interviews with hip-hop artists, for example, Kembrew McLeod (1999) identifies six support claims to being authentic that these artists used in order to differentiate themselves from outsiders or "poseurs" and "wannabes." These auxiliary characteristics of being authentically hip-hop were being black rather than white, supporting underground rather than commercial artists, being true to oneself rather than following mass trends, being hard and acting masculine rather than being soft and feminine, coming from the urban streets rather than from the suburbs, and being able to connect one's participation to old-school hip-hop rather than to the new mainstream form of commodified hip-hop. Authenticity claims—in other words, claims to being a true hip-hop artist and a valued insider rather than an inauthentic pretender—were situated in relation to these characteristics. Authenticity discourses are important within subcultures that differentiate themselves from the privileged dominant or mainstream culture: they are important both for defining the fault lines between these subcultures and the mainstream, and for limiting "true" and exclusive insider status to those who cross the authenticity threshold into full, celebrated membership. Individuals who fail to adequately perform an array of auxiliary characteristics are likely to be judged as inauthentic. But the performance of subcultural identity involves producing significant elements of the same presentational act, or playing the same status game as others. This creates some tension between authenticity as conformity and authenticity as individual expression. While oppositional subcultures construct a collective identity that is individualized and distinct from a conforming mainstream, they also produce a degree of sameness and conformity to the standards by which one establishes one's credentials as a member of an innovative oppositional subculture.

Navigating the tension between collective authenticity and personal authenticity is further complicated by the fact that being true to oneself is often among the auxiliary characteristics expected of members of many collectives when it comes to representing one's "realness" to the group. Among McLeod's hip-hop artists, for instance, being able to present oneself as someone who does his or her own thing and doesn't follow hip-hop trends is an important part of showing that one is authentically hip-hop. Artists do the things hip-hop artists have to do to show that they are authentically hip-hop at the same time as they must demonstrate that they are unique.

In his analysis of the fluid complexity of punk authenticity in a Florida punk scene, William Force (2009) similarly shows that punks constructed an authentically punk identity through the use of auxiliary characteristics such as owning records on vinyl, having unconventional hairstyles, and following expected punk fashions such as black t-shirts with the logo of a band, form-fitting Diesel-brand jeans, white leather belts, and hooded sweatshirts worn in combination with denim jackets with adorned patches. Punks adopted these styles to distinguish themselves from mainstream outsiders; but, equally importantly, many of these displays were fueled from within the local punk subculture (Force 2009: 291). They engaged in these distinction practices in order to "do" authenticities, in a comparative competition with other members of the scene subculture; doing subcultural performance correctly, consistently, and therefore "authentically," in adherence to internal hierarchies and established auxiliary characteristics of punk hipness, was standard practice. But, as with McLeod's hip-hop artists, it was also important to show one's authenticity by not appearing to try too hard to fit in and satisfy subcultural expectations. When stylized presentations of the auxiliary characteristics of punk appearance were everywhere in the scene, members pegged the expected in-group style as "the uniform"—a label meant as humorous derision. One local punk band reflects on the dilemma in its lyrics: "It used to be that I was one of a kind / It used to be that I would never fall in line / But now the kids they're kind of like me / Whatever happened to my identity?" (Force 2009: 300). This song indicates that attempts to display authenticity in the scene can undermine authenticity, if they seem scripted and contrived.

Rather than demonstrating a straightforward link between consumption style and authenticity, a key symbol of authenticity—the uniform—"could potentially signal inauthenticity dependent on the particulars of practice" (Force 2009: 300). Local punks awarded mock "scene points" and dismissed as "scenesters" people whose adherence to the stylized codes seemed too rigid. Thus scene members who wanted to be regarded as "authentic" engaged in a complicated style code that incorporated elements of the expected uniform, while using small modifications in the code or self-referential ironic distancing from the code in order to avoid being seen as the "hopelessly archetypical embodiment of [punk] fashion standards, one who [sub]scribes to them as if his or her social life depended on them" (Force 2009: 301). Navigating authenticity within both punk and hip-hop cultures requires conforming to subcultural expectations, but doing so in a way that appears natural and effortless rather than manufactured and contrived.

Negotiating one's authentic individual membership within a collective identity involves a balancing act between demonstrating commitment to the group through conformity to its codes and values and representing oneself as individually authentic. The need to make it appear as though meeting the subcultural expectations is natural and not manufactured is related to the difference between "being" an identity and "doing" an identity. Demonstrating that you don't even have to try to be hip-hop or punk indicates that you are hip-hop or punk at your very core, and not just playing with that identity as a temporary affectation.

Let us return to the idea that establishing personal authenticity within a group involves merging culturally negotiated ideas of belonging to that group with claims of individual uniqueness. The effective negotiation of the tensions between authenticity as a group member and the appearance of authenticity to oneself—and, hence, of independence from outside pressures to conform—is a balancing act that is especially visible in the formation of subcultural identities. Moreover, the difference between performing authenticity related to the collective and performing authenticity of the self can have very different implications for how we regard what counts as "keeping it real." Is one "keeping it real" by showing the signs of belonging in a community with a set of expectations about what it means to be real as part the group, or is one "keeping it real" by courageously being uniquely oneself in the face of a world that pressures one to be something else? These questions lead us to the complicated role of auxiliary characteristics in identity performances. One must display some shared characteristics of the group to keep one's claims to collective identity "real," while also not appearing to lack individual sincerity and "realness."

Doing versus Being: Identity Duration and Authenticity

Authenticating one's identity involves demonstrating that one is being true and not just performing the right auxiliary characteristics in order to blend in and be accepted. Williams (2006: 177) makes the following observation about the importance of being versus doing claims: "subcultural youth often talk about themselves in essentialist terms. For example, they regularly claim to *be* real, while charging others with simply *doing* subcultural things, such as dressing, speaking, or acting in certain ways in order to be cool or fit in." This essentialist idea—that one *is* the identity all of the time, and not simply performing it temporarily, within a group or context and for social approval—is important to authenticity claims. It is, furthermore, a critical component in inauthenticating (i.e. making inauthentic) the identity claims of others.

Within groups, asserting that a member is only temporarily enacting an identity represents a direct challenge to their authenticity. It suggests that they are not really, at their core, what they pretend to be. Examples of such inauthenticating statements abound. In her study of "real punks" and "pretenders," Kathryn Fox (1987) observed that subcultural insiders defined themselves as real punks because they lived their identities 24/7 and defined people who just "do" punk on weekends as inauthentic pretenders whose performances couldn't be sincere because they treated punk as a part-time identity job rather than as a full-time identity career. Charges of being "weekend warrior," "tourist," "part-timer," "wannabe," "pretender," "fair weather fan," "player" and the like question the commitment and depth of collective identifications for members who seem to move in and out of an identity without making it a stable, enduring piece of who they are. Arlene

Stein (1997) demonstrates, for example, how some committed long-term lesbians questioned the "true lesbian" identities of lesbian feminists whom they saw as adopting and performing those identities for political reasons. In their view, such women were "heterosexuals masquerading as lesbians," or heterosexual "lesbian tourists," on vacation from their real identities to engage in "ideological play." For them, the only "true" lesbians are lifelong lesbians whose identity is rooted deeply, who have never strayed from or merely dabbled in lesbianism, and whose desires, behavior, and identity have always been congruent with one another (Stein 1997: 162).

To bolster their durational authenticity credentials, individuals who make claims to an authentic collective identity often narrate stories of continuity over the life course, even in cases where they have only recently "discovered" or adopted a new identity. In her ethnographic fieldwork and interviews carried out among Pagan practitioners, Erin Johnston (2013: 560) observes that the central unifying logic of Pagan self-narratives was to emphasize that they had (re)discovered an underlying true self that had always been there. They did not view their transition to Paganism as a transformation of the self or as something new and different, but rather presented their exposure to Paganism as something that had prompted an "uncovering of their true, authentic selves that were previously hidden, forgotten, and not fully articulated" (Johnston 2013: 561). Thus claims to have realized that they had been a Pagan or Wiccan their entire life—or that, as one of Johnston's informants explained, "it's natural for me. So, it wasn't a choice, it was just it for me, that's all it is . . . that's who I am. It's part of my DNA, if you will" (Johnston 2013: 561)—were designed to show that Pagan identity was a central, permanent, natural, essential part of who they are.

Essentialism imbues identity with a natural, inherently biological quality that guarantees its realness. While Johnston's informant was likely using DNA as a metaphor for how deeply etched the identity feels, the use of biological essentialist metaphors to describe adopted, chosen identities illustrates how strongly authenticity claims are tied to life course duration. Demonstrating that this is always who one has been leaves the identity less open to question than if it appeared to be temporary, mutable, subject to social pressures, impermanent, and fleeting.

That some members of voluntary groups such as Pagans and punks narrate essentialist claims to *be* an identity rather than just do or choose it demonstrates the powerful quality of durational vocabularies of motive associated with having a core aspect of the self that is also permanent. While to outsiders to such sub-cultures the claim to an essential and permanent core rather than a chosen and therefore potentially mutable element may seem unusual, to insiders this durational vocabulary of motive seems natural and reinforces both their sense of belonging and their authentic commitment to the group's identity. Subcultures are, of course, social constructions rather than core essences, but this is also true of many types of group identities that are less volitional and thus appear more natural. Battles over identity authenticity also occur in the more subtly social constructed cases of ethnicity, race, and nation. Unlike subcultures, elements such as ethnicity have been historically treated by many societies and their mem-bers as essential and biological attributes rather than arbitrary or socially constructed (Williams 2019: 610). Nonetheless, establish-ing authenticity requires a social authentication of elements that are assumed to be rooted in something real such as blood, ances-try, or connection to region, land, or place.

Authenticating National, Ethnic, and Racial Identities

How do we demonstrate that we are authentically Scottish, Native American, Latino/a, or black? How do we make claims to be nationally, regionally, ethnically, or racially authentic? As we saw in the introduction, Italian pop star Mahmood's authentic-ity as an Italian was questioned by a deputy prime minister who used a narrow set of auxiliary characteristics to define national authenticity: that set largely excluded "foreigners" whose *recent* ancestry could be traced to other countries, especially if that ances-try was not ethnically Italian. Debates over national, ethnic, and racial authenticity often revolve around membership requirements related to what auxiliary characteristics count and how much each one weighs. Here again, duration (the enduring nature and rela-tive permanence of the identity) and density (visibility markers and intense performances of the identity) factor into the debate.

In their analysis of Scottish national identity, Richard Kiely and co-authors (2001) examined national identity construction and maintenance through interviews with more than a hundred owners of large estates and farms in Scotland and more than a hundred administrators and directors of cultural organizations based in Scotland. They focused on *identity markers* and rules that people use, defining the former as any characteristics that one presents to others in order to support an identity claim and that others will consider in validating that claim. Such markers may include place of birth, ancestral heritage, commitment to a place, accent, and dress (Kiely et al. 2001: 36). Kiely and colleagues outlined claim, attribution, and the receipt of claims and attributions as the key national identity processes, demonstrating that people used a mix of identity markers and rules. Some of these markers, for example accent, are treated as fixed, while others, for example place of residence and dress, are treated as fluid. Some fixed markers are easily accessible to observers of one's identity performance (e.g. accent), while other markers are less immediately accessible (e.g. place of birth). Likewise, some fluid markers of identity (dress, place of residence) are easily accessible to observers, while others (length of residence) are somewhat less accessible. These markers get attached to "rules of claim" that assess identity on the basis of the relative weight of markers. One challenge faced by people claiming a Scottish national identity is that easily accessible markers, by virtue of this accessibility, often hold more interactional weight than ancestry and place of birth, even though these latter categories, if they were visible, might be given more weight, since they demonstrate the naturalness and longevity of one's identity. That is, despite having access, in principle, to birth and ancestry to support their claim to being authentically Scottish, many Scottish-born elites had their Scottish identity challenged because their upbringing and education had afforded them English accents.

As we have seen in the case of duration concerns over authentic subcultural identity, markers treated as fixed (whether they actually are fixed or not), for example place of birth, place of upbringing, ancestry, accent, physical appearance, and name, often have more weight than markers treated as fluid and thus subject to change, such as dress and place of current residence. One could, however, make a tentative claim for Scottish identity if one has spent a significant number of years living in Scotland and thus demonstrated a seemingly stable and enduring commitment to Scottish identity.

The presence of identity markers and rules is also visible in ethnic authenticity claims. Disputes over Native American or Latina/o identities in the United States often center on authenticity claims tied to various expected auxiliary characteristics such as physical appearance, residential location, and language. Joane Nagel (1994: 160) notes that, even when ancestry can be documented, doubts can arise about the cultural depth (and therefore density and authenticity) of the individual's ethnicity or ethnic identity; these doubts are manifested in questions such as whether a prospective Latina/o speaks Spanish, or whether a potential candidate for an American Indian identity was raised on a reservation or in the city. Eva Garroutte (2003) shows that whether one "does American Indian identity" well enough to be considered authentic is tied to both the apparent naturalness and the timing and consistency of the performance; people who have recently discovered or are exploring their Native American or American Indian identities but cannot point to a long history of "being American Indian" as evidence of "doing American Indianness" for decades often raise the issue of "ethnic fraud" or "playing American Indian." Such individuals are accused of *ethnic switching*, of being "new American Indians" or "born-again American Indians" (Garroutte 2003: 85–6). The terms "new" and "born-again" suggest a durational starting point to the identity that casts upon it a lack of legitimacy by comparison to the identity of someone who has been American Indian for a lifetime and whose starting point is biological birth rather than some recent "optional play." Reclaimers who have come to self-identify as American Indian only recently attempt to challenge permanence as a measure of authenticity and instead depict a form of authenticity based on the intensity of doing identity work through the adoption of specific values and practices associated with "being American Indian" (see Jacobs and Merolla 2017). They make identity authenticity claims or "authenticating moves" that are based on demonstrating an identity by the intensity (density) of doing rather than the permanence (duration) of being.

The linguist Petra Shenk analyzes how bilingual Mexican American women, college students in the same group of friends, made *authenticating moves* to legitimate their Mexican ethnic identity and to simultaneously challenge or inauthenticate the identity of their peer rivals; and they did this in conversations with one another. As friends, the participants regularly marked their ethnic heritage in conversations, directly and indirectly, and referenced these things in relation to their racialized selves (Shenk 2007: 198–9). They regularly debated each other's degree of "Mexicanness" using a mixture of ethnic, national, and racial criteria. In the context of their conversations, they exploited three ideological constructs, namely purity of bloodline, purity of nationality, and Spanish linguistic fluency, to navigate ethnic authenticity linguistically and interactionally. While they discursively constructed their ethnic identities through larger dominant discourses that established the ideological prerequisites for Mexicanness (pure blood, birthplace, and fluency in the Spanish language) they also mobilized and played with these ideologies in complex and local-relationship-specific ways within their group and showed identity to be negotiable and contingent.

Authenticity is a theme related directly to multidimensionality, as well as to fluidity and the mobility of social and collective identities. A number of ethnographic studies of how people navigate their ethnic or racial identities in specific contexts help to illustrate this point.

Racial authenticity is performed to gain symbolic status within groups. Prudence Carter (2003) draws from a sample of low-income African American youths aged between 13 and 20 in Yonkers, New York, to analyze how young African Americans position themselves through the presentation of their black identity. Carter shows that the youths in her sample maintain "authentic" black identities through auxiliary characteristics such as using black youth speech codes, wearing the appropriate clothing, listening to the proper music, and walking with a specific gait. They set symbolic boundaries to ward off outsiders, to gain status among group members, and to evaluate "which of their co-ethnics was most worthy of 'black' cultural membership based on their use of specified resources" (Carter 2003: 142). Judging one another's legitimacy as "real" black persons involved constructing and policing the category requirements of "authentic blackness." Peers policed the auxiliary characteristics of "being black" and, in cases where people lacked "black" cultural authenticity and employed "white" cultural markers, that cost them the status of authentic group members. Carter develops the term *black cultural capital* to explain the cultural competencies and currencies that African American youth needed in order to successfully perform black identities. Bourdieu (1984) used the term *cultural capital* to show how people use styles, tastes, preferences, cultural knowledge, and attitudes to exclude others and to limit access to high-status groups or institutions. Cultural sociologists similarly use the concept of cultural capital when they look at cultural currencies and exclusion, primarily with a focus on how privileged individuals and groups employ culture to mark and enhance their exclusivity. Carter uses black cultural capital to highlight the importance of context-specific forms of cultural status and value. Thus, for example, while listening to classical composers like Beethoven and Mozart would serve as identity-reinforcing cultural capital in the context of being among older members of the white upper-middle and upper classes, listening to rap or hip-hop, not classical music, serves as the positively valued, identity-reinforcing cultural capital for black youths navigating their status position among their peers.

Ideas such as "black cultural capital," "youth subcultural capital," and "gay cultural capital" are useful analytic tools to remind us that what styles, tastes, and cultural repertoires are valued for conferring inclusion and status is context- and identity-dependent. Various forms of cultural capital or *cultural currencies* are summoned toward the goal of achieving status and authenticity. As Carter (2003) demonstrated, African American youths deployed dual cultural capital by using black cultural capital in peer settings and code-switching to dominant cultural capital in mostly white middle-class settings or in interactional contexts such as white-dominant workplaces or interactions with white adults in mostly white institutional settings.

Natasha Warikoo (2007) analyzed racial authenticity among second-generation youth in the multiethnic settings of New York and London. Warikoo found that both in-group and out-group peers expected others to conform to behavioral scripts associated with their racial identity. Indo-Carribeans, for instance, sanctioned their co-ethnic peers for listening to rock or grunge music associated with "white" tastes. Warikoo observes that, while children of immigrants in multiethnic neighborhoods are increasingly multidimensional in their identities, they still frequently rely on behavioral and consumption scripts about essential racial and ethnic qualities in assessing the authenticity of the racial and ethnic identities of their peers.

Authenticity in Organization and Place Identities

It is not just individuals who strive to gain status by "being" or appearing to be authentic. Collective entities such as organizations and places also make authenticity claims. Carroll and Wheaton (2009: 256–7) argue that organizations are especially important to the construction of authenticity; organizationally constructed images of authenticity, they argue, "gain more attention, gather stronger appeal, convey better credibility and persist longer than those which are not effectively organizationally embedded." Using the organizational construction of authenticity in the US food and dining industry as a case study, they emphasize a distinction between *type authenticity* and *moral authenticity*. Type authenticity indicates that something is true to its type (or genre, or category). For example, is it an authentic barbecue joint, or an authentic steakhouse, or an authentic Jewish delicatessen, or an authentic sushi restaurant? Moral authenticity indicates that something is true to the sincere beliefs of those involved; that is, it is true to itself rather than to its type. For example, the early Ben & Jerry's ice-cream company, with its quirky uniqueness and its emphasis on a social mission, was seen as satisfying the criterion of moral authenticity. Relatedly, Carroll and Wheaton argue that each of these forms of authenticity has spawned unique, albeit related, new forms of authenticity, which they label *craft authenticity* (if something is made using the right methods and ingredients) and *idiosyncratic authenticity* (if there is a commonly agreed upon quirkiness to the product or place, often backed by a historical reputation).

Notable about these types of organizational authenticity is that they map very well onto the same tensions that individuals use to construct identity authenticity. As discussed previously, individuals often strive for both authenticity to a type (am I authentically black, Native American, punk, or Pagan?) and authenticity to a sincere, idiosyncractic, unique moral self (am I unique, not subjected to group pressures to be something I am not, and am I true to myself?). While organizations and individuals are quite distinct types of entity, they have much in common with respect to the central tensions in how they construct identities.

Another similarity between individuals and organizations is that they both engage in impression management strategies. Goffman (1959) developed the concept of impression management to describe the ways in which individuals manage how they present themselves to others in order to create the desired impression of who they are. Impression management involves displaying the right cultural competencies and cultural markers to present oneself as authentic within the limits of the performance one is engaged in, be that a performance of one's category membership or a performance of one's unique idiosyncratic sincerity. Organizational performances of idiosyncratic authenticity, for example, rely on key cultural markers of sincerity and tradition to construct one's organization or brand as authentic and its products distinct from mass-produced and therefore inauthentic products. Johnston and Baumann (2007) argue that the organizational frame of authenticity includes social constructions of authenticity as tied to such features as the perception of sincere expressions, removed from conscious calculation and strategy, creation by hand rather than industrial manufacture, local flavor, anti-commercialism, closeness to nature, and distance from institutional power. Thus, in the luxury wine business, for example, Beverland (2005) demonstrates that a focus on handcrafting techniques and the disavowal of commercial motives and rational production methods are strategies of constructing brand authenticity that maintain the valued status of a brand as authentic and thus coveted in a commercial marketplace where consumers are interested in purchasing authenticity. Growers and merchants play up the notion that they still use traditional methods of making wine, while downplaying or obscuring the many industrial processes that they have added to produce the wine in larger quantities for the sake of larger sales. Much as Goffman's analysis of impression management highlights the sometimes cynical and strategic performance of self to others, presentations of brand and organizational identity can be strategic in attempting to appear sincere. Presenting authenticity through the appearance of being above commercial concerns is often, ironically, a market strategy deeply connected to commercial incentives.

In addition to promoting impressions of idiosyncratic or personal authenticity and sincerity, organizations, just like individuals, also present type authenticity with respect to the various categories they belong to. One can examine, for example, how they use auxiliary characteristics, in-group and out-group comparisons, and cultural scripts of authenticity to perform ethnic identities. Many "ethnic" restaurants, for example, will strive to demonstrate that they are authentically Italian, Chinese, or Mexican. Lu and Fine (1995: 535) note that market transactions at art galleries, festivals, restaurants, music venues, and clothing stores are some of the means by which ethnic groups make their ethnicity "real" to others. Looking specifically at Chinese restaurants, they explore how constructing authenticity is a fluid, hybrid negotiation between an ethnic organization and its clientele. As they conducted their research in a small city (Athens, Georgia) without a significant Chinese American population or a densely concentrated urban enclave called "Chinatown," Lu and Fine found that constructions of the "authentically Chinese" restaurant involved a modified, diluted, and Americanized version. The navigation of Chinese ethnic authenticity was thus locally produced; and the rules for authenticity are different in small southern US cities from what they are in China or in New York's Chinatown. Authenticity is an identity resource wherein the auxiliary characteristics are not entirely stable and change according to specific contexts and in relation to specific audiences. A major reason why consumers in Athens sought out Chinese restaurants was that the food is different and fits a specific type of request, for ethnic as opposed to generic, ethnically unmarked food. Demonstrating authenticity required emphasizing difference, but difference also needed to be modified to suit local perceptions of Chinese food and décor. In short, the ethnic restaurant in a non-ethnic enclave must appear to be distinctive and "ethnic," but also remain sufficiently similar to other restaurants in its core characteristics to promote acceptance and to appeal to clients who seek a specific kind of authentic experience.

Marie Gaytan (2008) examines the accomplishment of ethnic authenticity among Mexican restaurants in four small New England cities and finds, similarly, that the accomplishment of ethnic authenticity is a negotiated, local, and social construction. One characteristic that both Gaytan and Lu and Fine found is that the ethnic appearance and role performance of waitstaff and cooks were important to an organization's claims to authenticity. In

New England, for instance, customers expected the employees of "authentic" Mexican restaurants to be Mexican, and challenged the authenticity of businesses where the employees looked white or spoke only English and could not speak Spanish. Gaytan (2008: 321) notes that the vast majority of Spanish-speaking staff were from El Salvador and not Mexico, but were coded as contributing to the place's being authentically Mexican because their Hispanic appearance and Spanish language fluency allowed them to pass as Mexican in a way a white college student server from Northampton in Massachusetts could not.

Gaytan highlights a distinction between commemorative authenticity and Americanized authenticity. *Commemorative authenticity* emphasizes a connection to traditions located in Mexico and ties the "essence" of authenticity to the original region, its practices, and its people. Restaurant owners who strived to achieve this kind of authenticity often had to compete with New Englanders' perceptions of Mexican authenticity that were rooted in familiarity with popular Americanized Mexican foods and types of décor. One owner complained, for instance, that a local magazine published a lukewarm review that praised his food but commented on the "lack of Mexican charm" in the ambiance: it didn't have sombreros and piñatas, which they associated with an amplified symbolic presence of "Mexicanness." *Americanized authenticity* refers to a hybrid form of authenticity. Recognizing that the strangeness of absolute and unadulterated commemorative authenticity presents significant commercial challenges (e.g. Americans won't like the spices and seasonings of actual Mexican dishes; Americans expect tortilla chips as a part of authenticity because they associate them with Mexican restaurants, and thus with Mexican traditions), many restaurants fashion a more safely marketable authenticity— still recognizably different and ethnic, but comfortably so—that appeals to the local region as well as to the commemorative, traditional homeland. Managers of restaurants expressed the view that the local region shaped their presentations of authenticity; thus one owner explained that his restaurant is "too Americanized" for Californian palates and notions of authenticity, but is sufficiently Americanized for New Englanders, who have less pure and more diluted integrative demands in the area of authenticity. Among the strategies that Mexican restaurants used in New England in order to establish a localized Mexican authenticity was to emphasize some traditional cultural elements, while also catering to New England customer demands and illusions about Mexican food. Offering "mesquite-grilled" salmon, for example, blended traditional Mexican flavoring with a non-traditional Americanized entrée popular in New England (Gaytan 2008: 332).

The construction of ethnic authenticity in food industries is an interesting case for understanding debates about the authenticity of identity and the connections between identity authenticity and multidimensionality and mobility. While authenticity is seen as a stable and enduring core of identity, it is also continuously negotiated according to our social relations, our interactions with others, and the contexts and environments we operate in. Just as, in their construction of personal ethnic identities, individuals develop context-specific authenticity and inauthenticity claims, for themselves and others, organizations, too, navigate ethnic identities where authenticity becomes a moving and partly malleable target, based on the configuration of environments and relations that shape the formation and maintenance of identity claims. Because authenticity is complicated by the multifaceted dimensions of socially defined identity categories, and because it is constructed in relationships that are themselves multidimensional and in constant flux, it is important to explore how authenticity is managed with respect to the many complementary and competing elements of identity and to analyze how authenticity changes across different environments.

Further Reading

Turner, Ralph. 1976. "The Real Self: From Institution to Impulse." *American Journal of Sociology* 81(5): 989–1016.

A classic in the study of the self, Turner's piece distinguishes between people who connect self-authenticity or their "real self" to institutional demands in order to control their behavior, and people who find self-authenticity or their "real self" in acting upon their impulses, free from institutional constraints.

Force, William. 2009. "Consumption Styles and the Fluid Complexity of Punk Authenticity." *Symbolic Interaction* 32(4): 289–309.

Force ethnographically explores constructions of authenticity in the punk scene, demonstrating that authenticity is fluid and negotiated. He highlights the delicate balance between demonstrating commitment through conforming to group standards and representing oneself as an original individual.

Garroutte, Eva. 2003. *Real Indians: Identity and Survival of Native America*. Berkeley: University of California Press.
Garroutte analyzes the construction of authentic "real [American] Indian" identities, exploring the various legal, biological, and sociocultural authentication dimensions that are battled over in debates over authenticity and inauthenticity.

Jacobs, Michelle R., and David M. Merolla. 2017. "Being Authentically American Indian: Symbolic Identity Construction and Social Structure among Urban New Indians." *Symbolic Interaction* 40: 63–82.
An interesting companion to Garroutte's book, Jacobs and Merolla's study analyzes the strategies that "urban new Indians" use to authenticate their American Indian identities in the face of skepticism occasioned by their lack of legal criteria for authenticity.

Carter, Prudence L. 2003. "'Black' Cultural Capital, Status Positioning, and Schooling Conflicts for Low-Income African American Youth." *Social Problems* 50(1): 136–55.
Carter demonstrates the performance of racial authenticity through the strategic deployment of black cultural capital to perform black identities. She shows that African American youths develop cultural currencies to navigate both dominant institutional and non-dominant African American interactional contexts.

Carroll, Glenn R., and Dennis Ray Wheaton. 2009. "The Organizational Construction of Authenticity: An Examination of Contemporary Food and Dining in the US." *Research in Organizational Behavior* 29: 255–82.
Using the US food and dining industry as a case study, Carroll and Wheaton examine organizational constructions of authenticity, emphasizing the distinction between type authenticity (being true to the genre) and moral authenticity (appearing sincere).

Lu, Shun, and Gary Alan Fine. 1995. "The Presentation of Ethnic Authenticity: Chinese Food as a Social Accomplishment." *Sociological Quarterly* 36(3): 535–53.
Lu and Fine use Chinese restaurants in a small southern city as a

case study, to explore how ethnic authenticity is a fluid, hybrid negotiation, between organizations and their clients. Ethnic authenticity was interactionally produced through local cultural rules for authenticity that differ from the rules found in New York City's Chinatown or in China.

Gaytan, Marie Sarita. 2008. "From Sombreros to Sincronizadas: Authenticity, Ethnicity, and the Mexican Restaurant Industry." *Journal of Contemporary Ethnography* 37(3): 314–41.

Gaytan explores the accomplishment of ethnic authenticity among Mexican restaurants in four small New England cities, demonstrating that ethnic authenticity is negotiated and accomplished locally in interactions between the organizations and their clientele. They highlight a distinction between commemorative authenticity tied to the original region (Mexico) and a hybrid "Americanized authenticity."

4

Multidimensionality, Intersectionality, and Power

Identity and Social Inequalities

Identities are often portrayed as relatively coherent. The concept of a group or collective identity, in its very categorization and iteration, conveys at least an assumption of some important sameness within the category. This notion of categorial identities as coherent formations can, however, cause problems of stereotyping, overgeneralization, and oversimplification of complexity. Social categories are diverse and multidimensional but the cognitive shortcuts we employ, through our culturally shaped perception, often reduce diverse categories to rather unidimensional images. To illustrate this, let us start with the concept of generational identity, which suggests that members of a generation are a relatively coherent category with similar experiences, worldviews, and personalities.

Twenty-first-century news stories about millennials as a generational category with tolerant attitudes, but also spoiled by entitlement and by a strong streak of narcissism, are commonplace. Millennials, we are told, have been damaged by the abundances of modern technology and by an active parenting style, and are inclined to make lifestyle choices that delay the responsibilities of adulthood. These stories about the collective identity of millennials (the generation born roughly between 1981 and 1996, though often extended by some to include the opening years of the millennium) are instructive for how we think about identity. More often than not, the portrayal of millennials in these stories conjures up an image that is not representative of the full range of the people born between the landmarks of 1981 and 1996. In a provocative editorial entitled "Attention, Millennials: The Real World Is Not a 'Safe Space,'" Tom Sileo writes:

> Instead of whining and retreating to "safe spaces," wouldn't it be nice if more college students dedicated some of their time, energy and intellect to supporting the men and women of our military community? After all, they are the ones fighting to keep ISIS and al Qaeda terrorists out of your imaginary "safe spaces." Nobody cares about your feelings, millennials. It's time to grow up and be thankful for your freedom. (Sileo 2016)

In criticizing millennials as sheltered, privileged college students divorced from the real world and having little interest in supporting the military, the writer produces a fairly narrow vision of what millennials are. While some millennials attend college, most of them do not, and some in fact serve in the military. Upon reflection, it is obvious that a group as large and diverse as all the people in the world born between 1981 and 1996 cannot be coherently defined by a single set of universally shared characteristics. Yet implicit portrayals of millennials as relatively undifferentiated and unidimensional are widespread. Education scholar Fred Bonner notes that the traits emphasized in millennial portrayals apply primarily to "white affluent teenagers who accomplish great things as they grow up in the suburbs, who confront anxiety when applying to super-selective colleges, and who multitask with ease as their helicopter parents hover reassuringly above them" (Hoover 2009). In talk of millennials, white college students often come to stand in for a category that is full of non-college students and that is diverse both in race and in class. Assigning naming to generations and creating other large categories of collective identity invites broad generalizations, which fit some members better than others. Identity categories that we often treat as coherent are incredibly diverse and multifaceted, be they generational identity, racial identity, sexual identity, subcultural identity, or gender identity. This diversity is often lost in the process of categorization; *which* members of the group come to be seen as representative of the category is linked to cultural privilege.

To understand the analytic importance of multidimensionality within individual and collective identities, it is worth considering the relationship between *accented particularization* of the marked (the process of emphasizing marked differences) and *unaccented universalization* of the unmarked (the mental habit of leaving unmarked privilege in the background). Social marking is an asymmetrical process of cultural cognitive classification wherein we actively *stress* one side of a relational contrast as socially specialized or category-specific (the marked) while mostly ignoring the other side as generic and unspecific (the unmarked) (Brekhus 1996: 500). In other words, we cognitively *particularize* the marked while implicitly *universalizing* the unmarked. The most heavily marked categories are often cognitively perceived as master statuses that not only differentiate the marked from the general, the standard, or the "normal" but afford it a heightened salience, which crowds out, or washes over, the social relevance of unmarked statuses. Unmarked categories, by contrast, are perceived as undifferentiated from the generic standard and thus frequently come to serve as the default—as non-inclusive representatives of the universal. We often see members of marked categories as being more heavily defined by their socially marked attributes than by any unmarked attributes they have, although those also comprise who or what they are. Thus, for example, a 104-year-old white man is more likely to be defined and described by his age than by his race, while a 36-year-old black man is more likely to be defined and described by his race than by his age.

Both accented particularization and unaccented universalization divorce identities from their multidimensionality. Accented particularization of marked categories elevates the categories in question to master status, thereby effectively reducing a collective or an individual to marked categorial features and limiting the consideration accorded to unmarked attributes. Unaccented universalization, on the other hand, robs categories of their multidimensionality by implicitly reducing the whole category, all its individual members, to unmarked, "generic" specimens. Accented particularization of millennials, for example, defines a diverse group by its marked generational identity and those auxiliary characteristics associated with millennials, while unaccented universalization also tacitly selects millennials who are unmarked on dimensions other than generation and makes them stand in as "generic," and therefore "typical," millennials. A similar phenomenon occurs with other marked categories. Many portrayals of "the gay community" for example, pick up gay identity as the key marked attribute of gay people. Accenting "gay" as the attribute to focus on often leads to an uncritical assumption that "gay" is the only thing that matters, so that other dimensions of identity such as race, age, sex or gender, and class fade from active consideration. Gay middle-class white men come to stand in as generic representatives of the gay community. Thus lesbians, working-class gay men, gay men of color, and other members multiply marked become special cases or variations from a "standard."

The multidimensionality of collective identities is also reflected in individual self-identities. Just as collectives are diverse, stratified, and differentiated, individuals' constellations of identity characteristics are multifaceted, hierarchically organized, and differentiated. Dimaggio's (1997: 274) distinction between studying identities as collectives and studying the collective categorial elements in self-identities reminds us of the close relationship between how categories are organized in the social world and how they are reorganized in the cognitive world of individuals. The relationship between collective identities and self-identity and between complexly organized societies and complexly organized selves is important. One criticism of Mead and earlier theorists of the self is that they saw society as relatively unified and the self as fairly "generic" and general. Stryker and Serpe (1982: 206) point out that Mead viewed society as a relatively undifferentiated cooperative whole and that, in consequence, symbolic interactionists in the Mead tradition often adopted a conception of the self as a singular, global, undifferentiated whole. This trend is further exacerbated by a focus on micro, face-to-face interaction that can contribute to an overemphasis on agency and to ignoring relatively enduring social structures. Stryker and Serpe point out that in a complex social structure where people have diverse and multiple roles the self is multifaceted. Their views share similarities with Simmel's idea that the individual is shaped by the web of his or her multiple group or role affiliations; thus Stryker and Serpe bring out the complex character of socially constituted selves, differentiated as they are according to their multiple roles.

Conceptions of self-identity can miss the multidimensionality of the self, either by assuming an unmarked generic universal self (as Mead did) or by assuming a totalizing marked self or master status—a model in which an individual with one marked status is assumed to be nearly entirely defined by that marked attribute. Identity theorists have developed multidimensionality and intersectionality as themes in reaction to previous scholars' unidimensional conceptions of self-identity, which have often implied the universal standpoint of a generic, unmarked human actor as a kind of social default. In part, Stryker's complication of Mead's overly universalistic idea of the self is a recognition that the self is made up of competing roles with different saliences and levels of power in different situations. The uniform view of a stable singular self, which develops in a cooperative society, has come under attack as social conflicts, genocides, mass protests, identity politics movements, intense nationalisms, and other contentious disputes between and within social groups have led many identity scholars to reject this view and its implications for identity. This power dimension becomes even more central as one recognizes that individuals balance a complex mix of identity attributes, which can include both marked and tacitly privileging unmarked statuses. A more focused interest in the multidimensionality of identities has also come about as sociology as a field has become more diverse and members of marginalized identity categories have drawn attention to the importance of non-universal, particularistic standpoints as well as to the problem of non-inclusive universalization.

Intersectionality and Multidimensionality: Challenges to Non-Inclusive Universalization

A cisgender Salvadoran American college student wakes up in the morning, kisses her girlfriend, and heads to work at her part-time job as a coffee barista. Having grown up in the suburbs in a family of modest income, she works toward paying for some of her college fees. Her identity is shaped by her race, her class, her sexuality, her age, and her occupation. What is she primarily? Is she a Salvadoran American, a Latina, a lesbian, a Latina lesbian, a woman, a cisgender person, a college student, a suburbanite, or a coffee barista? She is, of course, all of these things, but how do we view her and which of these attributes do we emphasize and consider most relevant to identifying her? And which ones does she regard as most central? The answer can vary greatly depending on the setting and on cultural sociocognitive assumptions of what is socially salient, what is taken for granted and unimportant, and what the social default is. She is too complex, as we all are, to be defined by a single label.

Scholars of identity have increasingly become interested in identity multidimensionality and its relationship to power and difference. Straying from the micro concerns of a research focused primarily on the process of identity internalization among "generic" social actors, identity theorists have become interested in the multiple attributes of stigma and privilege that people deploy or make salient depending on the structural environment and the social situation, and on how these are intricately related to power dynamics. *Intersectionality*, a term developed in anti-racist and feminist research, has become a popular orienting concept in the study of identity.

Legal scholar Kimberlé Crenshaw (1991) coined this term to emphasize the multidimensionality of marginalized subjects' lived experiences. Intersectionality emerged as a concept in critical race studies, a scholarly movement among legal scholars that challenges law's alleged neutrality, objectivity, and color blindness (Nash 2008: 89). Critical race scholars critique the notion that law responds to people objectively, as neutral "generic social actors" rather than as raced, classed, and gendered actors who operate within a society where race, class, and gender are important categorial axes that people use to judge and interpret actions. Responding to the exclusion of multiply marginalized subjects from theory and practice in feminist and anti-racist scholarship, Crenshaw and other intersectional scholars focus precisely on these subjects, who offer distinctive vantage points for observing the structuring of society.

Intersectional theorists give a multiple-vector twist to marginal standpoint theories. These multiple-vector approaches contrast earlier single-vector marginal standpoint theories, such as Hartsock's (1983) call for understanding the social world from a women's feminist standpoint. Intersectional theorists challenge the idea of a universalizing "women's standpoint," which ignores intra-group distinctions and implies a coherent perspective that is also implicitly coded as a western white women's standpoint. Single-vector standpoint theories place the accent on one position of marginality, and by doing this deemphasize other marginal vantage points and impose a non-inclusive universalization upon the vector in question. Crenshaw viewed intersectionality as a metaphor fit to evoke the "convergence among intersecting systems of power that created blind spots" in feminist and anti-racist activism (Hill Collins 2019: 26), more notably the hidden power of whiteness in feminism and of masculinist bias in anti-racist activism. Intersectionality regards race, class, gender, and sexuality as multiple axes that simultaneously interact with one another. A key contribution of intersectionality is that marginalized members cannot be defined or analyzed along a single axis of their marginality such as race or gender; these axes must be understood in conjunction with one another.

Intersectionality theory, with its roots in black feminism, has traditionally treated black women as the first group to study, because of their marginality on both race and gender axes (Nash 2008). In 2008, Jennifer Nash raised the question of whether, "in its emphasis on black women's experience of subjectivity and oppression, intersectional theory has obscured the question of whether *all* identities are intersectional or whether only multiply marginalized subjects have an intersectional identity." She argued that identities that are wholly or even partially privileged have generally been ignored, even though such identities, like multiply marginalized ones, are constituted by the intersections of multiple vectors of power. Nash (2008: 10) maintains that intersectionality has "generally been opposed to imagining non-multiply marginalized subjects as central to its theoretical project, particularly because of its investment in 'recovering' marginalized subjects' voices and experiences." Nash outlines the need for intersectionality to do more than address and describe multiple marginalizations; it should study how privilege and oppression intersect in informing any subject's experiences. Broadening in this direction would transform intersectionality from a theory of marginalized subjectivity into a generalized theory of the strategic deployment of marginalized and privileging identities. It is this general theoretical power of intersectionality that has attracted cognitive sociological theorists of identity multidimensionality.

While intersectional standpoint theorists have emphasized multiply marginal identities—and especially black women's standpoint (see Nash 2008: 8–9), given sociology's historical blind spots to the influences of race and gender—the analytic utility of thinking about multiple intersecting vectors that lead to different social perspectives from which to interpret reality, as Nash suggests, extends well beyond the multiply marginalized. It is, of course, important to understand marginality, but a sociology of identity, inequality, and intersectionality must also examine the other side of the marginality coin—normative privilege. Brekhus (1998) argues for a *sociology of the unmarked* that takes seriously examining the normative default categories and analytically marking all the elements of identity continua. Brekhus warns that focusing only on the marked, even when analyzed positively, reinforces an exaggerated sense of difference between marked categories and normative "default" categories and reproduces in our social analysis the markedness that already exists in social life. Nash argues that intersectional theorists too often imply that black women and the multiply marginalized are regarded as uniquely relevant to their theories. The situation reproduces what Brekhus (1998: 38–9) calls *epistemological ghettoes*, which bracket the marked as "non-generic" people, who are relevant to particularistic theories about their unique subjectivities, but not to understanding generic principles of social reality; and it also reproduces the culture's epistemological blind-spotting of unmarked identity attributes. Both Nash and Brekhus note, however, the important potential implications of extending intersectionality theory beyond the examination and understanding of the multiply marginalized. A sociology of identity committed to understanding power and difference can analyze the full range of identity continua.

The blind-spotting of unmarked identity attributes in social research occurs both with respect to undertheorizing the normatively privileged sides of particular dimensions such as gender, race, and sexuality and with respect to analyzing axes of identity beyond the traditional set of race, class, gender, and sexuality. Scholars have generally assumed race, class, gender, and sexuality to be the most important dimensions of identity, but individuals in their daily lives do not always conform to scholarly assumptions about what dimensions of their social standpoint matter most. Identity attributes such as religious belief, occupation, political orientation, age, familial role (e.g. father, oldest sibling, grandmother, adoptive parent), moral self-identification, geographic lifestyle (e.g. rural, suburban, urban), passion and interest, and (sub)cultural practice often intersect to shape social standpoint, identification, and identity. Brekhus (2008: 1064) suggests that, in addition to feminist standpoint theories that emphasize gender,

Marxist standpoint theories that emphasize class, and intersectional feminist standpoint theories that emphasize the intersection of race and gender, we should also consider neo-Simmelian standpoint theories. Simmel (1969: 125–95) saw the modern individual as being the multidimensional product of overlapping social, religious, familial, ethnic, geographic, occupational, and other affiliations. The idea that one's self-identity is composed of multiple intersecting, overlapping, and competing affiliations that lead to a densely populated and heterogeneous self challenges a Meadean view of a single, generalized other. It also challenges concepts of identity that assume the dominance of any single identity membership, such as gender or race, in one's overall definition of self (Brekhus 2008: 1064). In my ethnographic research among suburban gay men, for example, I found that suburbanness, occupation, gender, class, race, and sexuality all intersected and shaped the identity presentations, identifications, and worldviews of the people I hung out with (Brekhus 2003).

Standpoint theorists, cognitive cultural sociologists, and interactionist theorists of "doing identity" have often worked in different traditions of different origins, but have much to offer one another. The idea of intersectional analyses developed in feminist and antiracist standpoint theories, the ideas of social markedness and unmarkedness developed in cognitive cultural sociology, and the ideas of identity as an interactional accomplishment developed in "doing identity" traditions work well in combination with one another. Our social selves are composed of competing privileging and stigmatizing attributes that correspond to various politics of inclusion and exclusion.

Marked and Unmarked: Accented Stigma, Hidden Privilege, and the Cognitive Politics of Social Identity

In October 2019, the University of Missouri's athletic department sent out a tweet celebrating the diversity of its student athletes. The tweet referred to two white women athletes under the captions "I am a future doctor" and "I am a future corporate financier," an African American woman athlete under the caption "I am an African American woman," and two African American men, one a staff member and one an athlete, under the captions "I value equality" and "I am a brother." In the tweet, the two white student athletes were defined by their career potential and aspirations, while the black student athletes and staffer were defined by such things as being African American or having values associated with diversity and equality. An attempt to allow racial pride, reduce color blindness, and celebrate diversity in its portrayal of students, the tweet ended up drawing horrified reactions because, by showcasing just one identity statement per person from much longer interviews and by choosing *this* pairing of subjects and qualifying attributes, the University of Missouri, a historically white institution, seemed to reveal a white culture-based tendency to view its black people first and foremost as raced subjects and its white people as generic human beings defined by their individual, yet *generally* human goals and aspirations. In the longer interviews from which these tweet captions were selected, the African American woman had mentioned that she was aspiring to be a physical therapist and the African American man pictured under the caption "I am a brother" had said that his most important quality was being a leader. Why, then, did these two captions not read "I am a future physical therapist" and "I am a leader"? And why did the captions for the white women not read "I am a white woman" or "I value equality"? The answer lies in the difference between how we generalize about marked and unmarked identity attributes.

Because we culturally perceive the social world unevenly— namely we notice and stress marked elements as socially specialized, while taking for granted unmarked elements as socially generic— we generalize differently from the marked and from the unmarked (Brekhus 1998). Thus, for example, black people are often perceived as racially specific humans, while whites are perceived as generic humans. In this context, African Americans are more easily defined than white Americans by their racial membership and by their commitment to values of diversity and equality (issues that are assumed to matter most to people defined as "diverse" and recognized as "unequal"). Whites are not typically defined by their whiteness or by their connections to diversity. Race and diversity are generally assumed to be issues of central importance to people in marked racial categories, but not to people in the default, "generic," "non-race-specific" category.

The power of the unstated is strong. Being defined as the normal, the unmarked, the standard from which others deviate is a privilege that frees people from having to think consciously about how a taken-for-granted attribute affects them. Consider, in the University of Missouri tweet, how the racially unmarked white athletes are defined by their career aspirations and potential (a potential they have fewer barriers to achieving, thanks to the socioeconomic advantage that has accrued to those with an unmarked category status), while the racially marked black athletes are defined by their marked attributes and by values related to these attributes. Notable here is that white people, as the unmarked, need not consciously think about their racial identity or about where valuing equality fits within their worldview (indeed, they experience unstated benefits from racial inequality). They may well express an interest in equality and diversity when asked about it, but, as the racial category that usually benefits from racial inequality, they can take their unequal benefits for granted and spend little energy considering how their value commitments around equality or inequality shape them and their opportunities. Richard Dyer (1988: 45) highlights the power of whiteness as an unmarked racial identity: "Power in contemporary society habitually passes itself off as embodied in the normal as opposed to the superior. This is common to all form of power, but it works in a peculiarly seductive way with 'whiteness,' because of the way it seems rooted, in commonsense thought, in things other than ethnic difference."

Constructing whiteness as bland, vanilla, boring, and average is itself a project of power. Suburban and Midwestern identities in the United States have often been associated with blandness and whiteness. Richard Rhodes (1987) described Kansas City as a land of "vanilla suburbs": a boring, unremarkable, bland, nondescript "everyplace" kind of place. The construction of blandness as power is not an accident. Kansas City developer J. C. Nichols created a racialized suburban landscape by placing restrictive covenants on deeds that prevented black people from living in residential suburban areas. These deed restrictions limited the options of non-whites to live in residential communities zoned to be distant from vice districts—that is, areas with few zoning restrictions and limited law enforcement on vice activities such as commercial sex, liquor sales, and gambling (Mallea 2019). Vice (at least that form of it that white society sees fit to police), color, and difference were all separated out from the ordinary,

colorless "vanilla" communities designed to be safe, uninterest-
ing, and unmarked. Developers in other US cities adopted similar
strategies for building and selling wholesome suburbia; as Amahia
Mallea (2019: 70) suggests, "Kansas City perfected and exported
vanilla." The metaphors of "vanilla" and "white bread" are two
metaphors frequently used to describe blandness and averageness,
and these metaphors are also white. Although blandness may have
a negative connotation in other contexts, assertions of identity
blandness are, typically, assertions of power and privilege. In my
ethnographic interviews of gay men in suburban New Jersey in
the 1990s, I was surprised by how many middle-class, suburban,
masculine, cisgender, white gay men proudly described themselves
as "ordinary," "plain," "bland," or "boring" (Brekhus 2003:
76). It became clear to me that these descriptions were popular
because they emphasized the many elements of an individual's
identities that were socially "normal" and therefore privileging.
Ruth Frankenberg (1993), one of the founders of whiteness studies, noticed that the white women she interviewed defined white
culture as "Wonder Bread" (a well-known brand of white bread),
by which they meant that it was ubiquitous but lacking in any
distinctive flavor. Defining themselves as cultureless, white women
saw difference either as positive cultural enrichment or as negative
vice, pathology, and danger. Their own culture, by comparison,
seemed to lack specific cultural value. Interviewing white youth
at two high schools (one predominantly white, the other multiracial), Pamela Perry (2001) similarly noted that white students
defined themselves as "cultureless" and as "not ethnic." Although
seemingly humble on the surface, the claim to be "cultureless" is
a measure of structural white racial superiority and dominance.

Dyer, Frankenberg, and Perry focus specifically on whiteness
and its seductiveness, but this pretense of ordinariness, as Dyer
suggests, is common to all forms of power; the strength of unmarkedness is its association with normalcy (see also Zerubavel 2018).
Whiteness serves as a particularly illustrative case, to demonstrate
that the key distinction is between marked difference and explicit
social value (negative or positive) on one side, and unmarked
"averageness" and implicit social value (unstated privilege) on the
other.

As individuals are comprised of multiple attributes that make up
their self-identities, we can think of these attributes as the various

ingredients that constitute one's recipe for the self. The marked ingredients are the flavors or spices that stand out as distinctive and specialized, while the unmarked ingredients blend into the background. Indeed, people with a mix of privileging unmarked attributes and potentially stigmatizing marked attributes often employ the language of blandness and lack of flavor (e.g. culture-less, plain, not ethnic, not specific) around their unmarked flavors, to argue against the dominance of their "spicier," marked flavors. Larger entities such as social movements may also highlight the ordinary composition of their more "respectable" and socially valued members, who set the overall flavor of the movement, as a way to offset the more "dangerous" flavors of marked difference, even as they lobby for some change that is based in part on difference. Individuals, social movements, neighborhoods, organizations, and nations make decisions around whether or not to emphasize the more socially marked and pronounced elements or to dilute markedness by highlighting generic commonalities and by rhetorically downplaying the power and flavor of the marked.

Deploying Markedness–Unmarkedness and Multidimensionality in Social Interaction

Individuals are multiply located socially; they have pluralistic selves and what Raphael (2017) refers to as *plural cognitivist identities*. A cognitively pluralist conception of identity highlights the managing of multiple competing attributes that draw different degrees of social value and cultural attention from others (Brekhus and Ignatow 2019: 9). Recall our previous example of a cisgender Salvadoran American college student, middle-class and lesbian, who works as a barista; all these identity attributes shape her lived experience, yet some are more likely than others to be perceived as defining elements of her identity, both by ordinary individuals and by social science analysts. One way to understand the multidimensionality of identity is to recognize that individuals use identity as a resource and deploy their competing identity attributes, marked and unmarked, in strategic ways.

How do people deploy identity as a multidimensional resource that balances their marked and unmarked attributes? Julie Bettie's (2000, 2014) intersectional analysis of class, race, and subcultural identities among girls at a California high school is instructive. Combining notions of doing identity with intersectionality, Bettie analyzed how high school girls do class identities and race or ethnic identities while simultaneously performing subcultural identifications and identities. A primary way for high school students to understand difference in their own ranks is through an informal peer hierarchy organized into cliques (Bettie 2014: 49). These cliques express subcultural styles that are structured along social class and racial and ethnic lines. Building upon Bourdieu's (1984) notion of habitus, which is the sum of our socially learned and unconsciously enacted dispositions, Bettie sees class and cultural difference as something embodied in the performance of the self. As Bourdieu (1984) has shown, tastes are associated with position in a social class structure; and they are relational (see also McLean 2017: 44–5). Tastes reflect status positions and are deeply intertwined with social value. Bettie illustrates the symbolic politics of dignity within a high school and shows that even the nuances of lipstick color are tied to larger issues of class, inequality, and symbolic boundary maintenance.

Bettie identified the main social class categories in the school as middle-class students and two types of working-class students. One type, "settled-living" students, came from families supported by relatively secure jobs and with modest homes. The other type, "hard-living" students, came from families supported by less stable, low-paying jobs and with chaotic, unpredictable living situations. Bettie observed that there was a general mapping of the school's clique structure; it consisted of the following groups, which were largely segregated on racial–ethnic and social class grounds. Among Mexican American students there were "Mexican preps," *las chicas* ("the girls"), and *cholas/os* ("hard cores"). "Mexican preps" were either middle class or working class, but aspired to be middle class. *Las chicas* were mostly from settled-living working-class families and hoped to attend vocational degree programs or community colleges. And *cholas/os* came from hard-living backgrounds and presented "tough" personas. Among white students, groups included "preps," "skaters" or "alternatives," "hicks," and "smokers" or "rockers" or "trash." "Preps" were middle-class students in the school's popular clique. "Skaters" or "alternatives" came mostly from working-class settled-living families. "Hicks" either were from farming families or showed an interest in agriculture. "Smokers" or "rockers" or "trash" were from hard-living backgrounds and developed oppositional cultural styles. Through these cliques and their embodied expectations, students expressed social class and ethnicity as subcultural taste. Bettie argues that a significant limitation in research is that little attention has been paid to class as a cultural identity that is performed. Thinking of class as an object of identity performance does not ignore its material dimensions but rather demonstrates how class is inter-actionally performed; class performances are an effect of social structure and a performance of social position (Bettie 2014: 51). Subculture itself becomes a class-based resource.

Amy Wilkins (2008) similarly examines the intersections of race, class, and gender in the identity projects of young women. Young people, she argues, use cultural symbols to resist aspects of the mainstream that they find constraining or are excluded from, and to establish group membership and belonging. They "use cultural resources, including gender, race, and class, to craft plans of action" (Wilkins 2008: 4). Wilkins explores three subcultures: Puerto Rican wannabes, goths, and evangelical Christians. These three identity projects were enacted by white women, to nego-tiate status hierarchies and solve problems. Goths transformed themselves from "geeks" into "freaks" and intentionally fash-ioned visibly marked identities for themselves as cultural deviants. They differentiated themselves from mainstream culture—their white middle-class culture of origin—by strategically positioning themselves as aesthetic, sexual, and emotional nonconformists. Navigating the intersections of stigma and privilege, goths both reject aspects of white middle-class culture (such as restraint in sexuality, in emotions, and in self-presentation) and use whiteness as a resource that reduces the status costs of their nonconforming presentations. Goths enact identity performances that are extreme but impermanent and afford them the ability to move between calculated marginality and a position of maintaining some of the advantages of middle-class white privilege. In particular, Wilkins examines how Goths negotiate the relationship between "cool" and "geeky." As studious, industrious, and technologically adept individuals, geeks are overinvested in adult middle-class values; but this very early commitment to mainstream adult values makes them socially and stylistically uncool in the school; hence they adopt and deploy "freak" Goth identities as a mediating category between their own geekiness and the school's cool (Wilkins 2008: 27). Displaying freakiness allows goths to access the valorized social visibility of coolness and carve out a marked social identity, yet without integrating the long-term social, cultural, and economic consequences of markedness. Theirs is a temporary marginalization, strategically chosen and based on subcultural affiliation, rather than a marginalization sedimented in a structural category beyond choice.

In contrast to the freaky cool of Goths, Christians in Wilkins's ethnography embodied casual, "ordinary," and "boring" versions of the self that emphasized being good, self-disciplined, and wholesome. Non-rebellious, Christians are perceived as "goody-goodies," "whitebread," and "vanilla" (Wilkins 2008: 96). Their boringness contrasts with the deliberately flashy displays of freaks and other visible youth subcultures. Taken in this sense, Wilkins argues, "boring" is the opposite of "cool" and indicates accepting and offering no challenge to, rather than symbolically contesting, the existing structure. Here the white middle-class social locations of most of the Christian students are not presentationally abandoned for more edgy, "dangerous" identities, but rather interconnected with presentations of conventionality and respectability. Although Christian students focus primarily on their identities as Christians and as "good people," these statuses are not separated from their intersectional race and class identities. The association of "whiteness" with "goodness" and "lack of vice"—discussed earlier with respect to "vanilla suburbs" being zoned and coded as safe, vice-free areas—applies as well to individual identities, where whiteness is associated with wholesomeness and vanilla. Christians regarded themselves as open and accepting, but they also enacted a system of meanings that cast them as culturally and morally virtuous, hence superior. Goodness and boringness and their relationship to the culturally unmarked play out in the reestablishment of cultural privilege.

Understanding the intersections and multidimensionality of identity is important in analyzing how power, privilege, and social inequalities are reproduced through various identity projects. Interactionist approaches to the self and to identity have often been criticized for lacking an interest in power; but recognizing the many ways in which people use power and privilege as discursive and presentational resources in daily interaction sheds light on power relations and on the social reproduction of inequalities. Moreover, while it is important to study the multiply marginalized, understanding power relations also requires analysis of the identity constructions of those who deploy privilege as a resource. The intersections of privilege and disadvantage provide a useful site for analysis. An intersectional understanding of how people deploy the privileging advantages of unmarkedness, its symbolic association with virtue, and its implicit social value involves studying not just youths, but adults as well. Analysts are attracted to the subcultural styles of young people, especially oppositional styles, yet subcultural performances of identity extend across all age groups.

While conducting research in the small town of Sumner, Missouri, Braden Leap (2017) heard rural white men of ages that ranged between 20 and over 80 tell survival stories from their trips to cities. In these narratives the men imagined themselves as "heroes of adventure plots that involved escapes from people of color, con artists, and homosexuals who supposedly made urban spaces perilous" (Leap 2017: 12). Among rural white men, masculinities are informed by the intersection of race, class, gender, sexuality, and region and by the discursive constructions of the rural–urban divide, even as rural communities are increasingly being physically linked with cities. These narratives, which associate manliness with whiteness, middle-class occupations, and heterosexuality, were fundamentally about identity. Without directly mentioning class or racial identities, these men created an ideal of rural masculine identity through survival narratives about urban areas imagined as places with "deviant" black men, homosexuals, and urbanites, against whom they defined themselves symbolically and morally (Leap 2017). Although never naming whiteness or rural maleness, their constructions of identity valued these things by defining cities as black, urban, untrustworthy, and dangerous. Rural men also portrayed the city as full of con artists; those ranged from pool sharks to shuttle drivers who expected tips and to lawyers and politicians who bent the rules to line their own pockets. The discursive representation of the city as a space overrun by selfish con artists from both the lower and the upper end of the class structure ensured that the only occupations worthy of respect were those associated with rural masculinity; there was no room for anyone outside this spectrum to make an honest living. Similarly, these rural men expressed their heterosexual identities by portraying urban areas as "dangerous" homosexual oases where the visible presence of gay males threatened to corrupt heterosexuality (Leap 2017: 18). Rural men's narratives about their trips to cities linked whiteness, masculinity, heterosexuality, and rurality. They combined their racial, sexual, and gender unmarkedness with rural identity to emphasize the racial, sexual, and gender markedness of many urban dwellers as a strategy for elevating their own identity.

Angela Stroud (2012, 2015) observes that white middle-class weapon-carrying men define themselves as "good guys with guns." An important part of this self-definition relies on the assumption that normative unmarkedness is good, and therefore on the implicit exclusion of poor black urban gun owners from full membership in the class "good guys with guns." Possession of a concealed gun is a practice shaped by race, class, and gender and by the cognitive frameworks good–bad and safe–dangerous, which define culturally marked racial and class categories as threats. Rural white men constructed for themselves a "good guy" identity that was attached to a notion of middle-class virtue reliant on the belief in community engagement and dependability. They depicted themselves as people who will stop to give aid to those in need (Stroud 2015: 109). Notably, however, assisting those in need applied only to the "good parts of town," where they saw commonality with people they believed could be trusted. In the "bad parts of town" concealed carry holders, much like Leap's rural men, "assume that those who claim to need help are setting them up to be victimized; instead of reaching out a hand, they are likely to reach for their gun" (Stroud 2015: 109). White gun owners' construction of themselves as "good people" was heavily tied to a white middle-class masculinity defined by involvement in the community—but with a very restrictive, in fact exclusionary definition of the latter.

Privilege, Identity, and Exclusion: Bullying and the Interactional Reproduction of Social Inequalities

Recognizing that identity is socially produced and intersectional sheds light on social problems such as bullying, aggrieved entitlement, and violence. While most exercises of privilege and exclusion are mundane and not physically violent, understanding violence as an extreme way of reinforcing elements of one's privileged identity demonstrates that identity work can take very strong forms of identity policing. People who exhibit bullying behavior often have high self-esteem but experience shame; turning violence onto others allows them to maintain this high self-esteem by directing attention away from their shame (Lamia 2010). People who bully are frequently from the unmarked category of social winners, not from the marked one of social losers in the status hierarchy of their school or society. Many bullies are disliked by some of their peers, but also seen as popular (Peeters et al. 2010: 1043). Bullies are often popular students from high-status peer groups (Pascoe 2013: 90); their victims are often from low-status marginalized groups. Frequent victims include obese students, LGBTQ students, and youths with disabilities (Pascoe 2013: 90). Average-build students bully obese students, youths who do not live with disabilities bully youths who do, and heterosexual cisgender students bully LGBTQ students. All this suggests that bullying often involves people in unmarked privileged categories who use violence to reproduce, interactionally, the symbolic boundary between socially privileged cultural insiders and socially disadvantaged outsiders. In many instances, the bully is making explicit the taken-for-granted status hierarchy of his or her environment by drawing attention directly to who the socially marked "status losers" are (e.g. overweight people, LGBTQ youths, youths with disabilities). In this sense, people who bully are not fringe pathological actors defying social norms, but socialized agents violently enforcing the normative status order. Their crime, in many schools, is not that they devalue some kinds of students, but that they do it so crudely, through physical violence rather than in the subtle ways in which others privilege majoritarian identity categories at the expense of marginalized ones. When state laws fail to protect LGBTQ and gender-variant people from discrimination and when airlines charge overweight people for an extra seat on flights, for example, they construct symbolic boundaries between marked categories and unmarked categories that reflect a status hierarchy that violent enforcers of the status quo can draw upon (Pascoe 2013).

In analyzing rampage school shooters, Kalish and Kimmel (2010) develop the concept of *aggrieved entitlement* to explain how young men with some privileging identity attributes (e.g. being men, being upper class or middle class, being white) engage in violence as an extreme form of social control and symbolic boundary maintenance, in response to a sense that they are not getting the full battery of privileges to which they believe their identity status entitles them. Some heterosexual men, for instance, feel entitled to having sexual access to women and engage in violence if they perceive their access to be blocked. Their violence reasserts societal male privilege as a form of inequality that should be fought for, while often also expressing shame over less privileging parts of their self (e.g. not living up to the standards of masculinity, being unathletic in a jock culture). In 2014, 22-year-old Elliot Rodger, a wealthy young man of mixed white and Asian American heritage, drove to a sorority house and shot three women, killing two of them, in a spree of violence that ended with his killing six people and injuring fourteen. His manifesto made it clear that he was angry that women rejected him and did not recognize him as the "supreme gentleman" by comparison to the men they dated. In addition to his strongly misogynistic views, he also lashed out at black and "full Asian" men, considering them undesirable by comparison with himself—a rich, half-white person; and he also raged against the more popular and more privileged full white and normatively masculine heterosexual men ("normies"). Rodger's act of violence is, at one level, an extreme outlier; but the intense identity distinctions he made (1) to assert his privileged identity attributes as a rich male and his partial privilege as half white, (2) to distance himself from less privileged groups (women, African Americans, Asian Americans), and (3) to direct anger at those elements of privilege he could not access (full normative or "normie" status) are instructive as to the most problematic and violent ways in which some people negotiate their attributes of identity privilege and stigma. And, while Rodger's act was an individual one, he has become the symbol for "incels"—a male supremacist online subculture whose adherents identify as "involuntarily celibate" because they perceive their male entitlement to sexual access as being thwarted and define themselves through hostile opposition to the women who reject them. To mark that they fall short of the masculine and societal privilege they aspire to, they refer to fully privileged men as "chads" (a name typically associated with white men, and in this context specifically with popular "alpha males") or "normies."

A parallel to individual forms of aggrieved entitlement operates at the collective level: terrorist organizations and some violent reactionary social movements are populated by people who feel a loss of privilege on some dimension of identity, while fiercely defending those aspects of identity privilege they still have (see Kimmel 2002). Bullying at the collective level often involves similar privilege-sustaining and stigma-shamed motivations as bullying at the individual level. The recent increase in "white nationalism" and in associated displays of bullying in the United States is driven by white participants (especially but not exclusively men) who are invested in narrowly policing the boundaries of Americanness. Many participants feel a loss of status on dimensions other than their whiteness. For some, their moderate social class position may be slipping as jobs disappear, or their rural heartland or rustbelt regions may be in economic decline in relation to more prosperous coastal cities. To maintain a sense of social value and privilege, they may assert and attempt to socially re-elevate their most enduring category of privilege: their race.

Markedness–Unmarkedness and Intersectionality in Regional Identities

The intersections of privilege and disadvantage also apply to regional identities. Rebecca Scott (2010) analyzes the cultural production of Appalachian identity and how its geographical character contributes to the construction of the region as a sacrifice zone. Representations of Appalachia as a region reaffirm its fundamental difference as an area suitable for sacrifice (Scott 2010: 32). Recurrent narratives of "white trash" throw Appalachia's poor whites outside the boundaries of respectable "whiteness" in a nation that codes wealth as white and poverty as black. Appalachia itself is coded as white, but as an exotic, marked "white," abnormal and distinct from boring, unmarked whiteness. Scott analyzes the intersections of gender and race in identifying three figures of mining masculinity: the family man, the tough guy, and the modern man. The family man is a heteronormative breadwinner and provider, with a wife and children; "he is symbolically white because the racially segregated labor market has historically reserved the family wage as a privilege of white men, which has helped ensure their status as national citizens" (Scott 2010: 72).

The tough guy is a hard worker, physically strong, brave, and he takes pleasure in the difficulty of his work. The modern man brings to the table a different kind of masculinity. He is in control of technology and able to dominate nature with modern machines and "forward-thinking" plans for economic development. He is impersonal, technological, and in tune with the trends of modernity (Scott 2010: 80).

Narratives about Appalachian masculinities combine ideas about rurality, region, masculinity, class, and race (whiteness) that are applied both to the people who use the land and to the land itself. Here whiteness and social class are multidimensional in ways that highlight both privilege and disadvantage. The construction of the liberal democratic citizen is tied to the privileging of abstract reasoning over the needs and limitations of the physical body, and in this context the coal miners and hillbillies of Appalachia are too close to nature and too removed from middle-class consumption patterns to fit into the modern, rational depiction of unmarked whiteness (Scott 2010: 109). This variety of whiteness that falls short of its modern, rational, unmarked counterpart extends into a collective regional identity in the Appalachian mountains—a rough-and-tumble rural landscape where white hillbillies and "white trash" are tied to an untamed nature, but where modern technology is taming the region and extracting its resources. Scott (2010: 80) highlights how the practice of mountaintop removal (MTR) mining is narratively constructed as an act of stripping the region of its markedness and making it more generic:

> MTR is constructed as a masculine technology of control against irrational and feminine-coded Appalachian nature ... By creating flat land, it allows West Virginia to overcome its crooked geography and become more like other parts of the United States. A common remark about reclaimed land is, "You wouldn't know you were in West Virginia!"

Scott adds that MTR proponents compare their mountaintop mining to the creation of housing developments, roads, and strip malls as activities that transform the landscape by homogenizing its terrains, and do so for general human benefit in the modern world and at the expense of natural local distinctiveness. An analysis of the construction of identity in Appalachia—both among its white residents and in the region as a collective entity—demonstrates the complex ways in which privilege and stigma combine in the formation of individual and regional identities.

The complexity of multidimensional self- and regional identities in intersection with one another is reflected in the work of scholars who examine the New South in America. Vanesa Ribas (2016) illustrates the complicated multidimensionality of intersectional identities among migrant Latina/o and African American slaughterhouse workers in the American South. More than just their racial identities, Latinas/os and African Americans, in the context of the slaughterhouse they worked at, negotiated racial identities that intersected with region, class, and migrant or native status in complex ways. While the larger racial hierarchy in the United States is constructed in such a way that African Americans are typically below Latinas/os, the status hierarchy in meatpacking plants of the American South is often complicated by the divide between the migrant status of many Latina/o workers and the native status of African American workers. Ribas (2016: 125) notes that, in the context of a workplace where Latina/o workers had a mixture of legal statuses, often possessed limited English proficiency, and were not "from here"—traits easily spotted by other workers and by supervisors on the shop floor—the fusing effect was to bring an otherwise heterogeneous group together by making it precariously employed and marginalized. Even though the special vulnerabilities of "illegality" touched directly only some migrants, the vulnerabilities associated with legal status radiated onto, and affected, the perception and standing of the "ethnoracial group" as a whole (Ribas 2016: 124–5). The precarious status of migrant Latinas/os also created a complicated identity for non-migrant African American workers, who, while of low status in general, could at least rely on the privilege of being natives. In most contexts in which native-born African Americans interact with other native-born United States residents, this feature constitutes an invisible aspect of African American identities; but it acquires salience in a context where marked "non-natives" are present and visible as a population. Despite the fact that blackness often retained a widely disparaged status both in the United States and in the migrants' countries of origins, many Latinas/os came to see it as a valuable resource in the workplace (Ribas 2016: 123). And, at times, it was an identity component that afforded African

Americans some protections against the vulnerabilities of illegality. In the packing plant, migrant Latinas/os often received the most undesirable physical labor jobs and avoided reporting injuries for fear of being fired and jeopardizing their ability to stay in the country. Many of the Latinas/os regarded African American workers as spoiled and lazy and thought that they were not required to work as hard as Latinas/os worked. The workers who felt this way often embraced a "tough guy" identity similar to that of Scott's (2010) white coal miners in West Virginia. Sometimes Latina/o migrants sought redress for their harsh working conditions by demanding that African Americans be exposed to oppressive labor conditions identical to theirs—a strategy that would bring them to the position of their more privileged co-workers by lowering that position rather than by improving their own circumstances (Ribas 2016: 132).

Few outside the immediate context of the meatpacking plant would consider being an African American slaughterhouse worker to confer a privileged identity, and yet these unusual nuances of privilege and marginalization remind us how complex and multifaceted identity is. The authority structure at the plant that Ribas studied had mostly whites in the upper management, but African Americans were often involved in mid-level supervisory positions in relation to Latina/o workers. Latinas/os were torn between grievances about work conditions that deteriorated for all, under a white superintendent, and racialized resentment of African American workers, who had a structurally more privileged position within these deteriorating conditions (Ribas 2016: 140). In this context, some Latina/o workers asserted that black workers (whom they often called *morenos*) received and gave one another preferential treatment because Latinas/os (*hispanos*) could be coerced into poorer working conditions as a result of the perception, often justified, that some lacked the documentation necessary for a legal status. In contrast to the strong views of Latinas/os about this relative privilege, African American workers often expressed sympathy for Latina/o migrants. They generally saw themselves as sharing with them the same experience of poor labor conditions and expressed a desire to work together with them. This sympathy was sometimes ambivalent; for example, African Americans understood why unauthorized migrants would take risks to survive, yet they also intimated that the law was the law and that violating it should have consequences. Much like other privileged racial categories in other contexts, they could express a self-identity of sympathetic understanding, while also defending legal practices that did not negatively affect them. Ribas suggests in conclusion that African Americans engaged in less intense boundary making because of their relatively advantaged position in the racial hierarchy of the workplace, a position assisted by their status as native, non-migrant Americans, even if African Americans rather than white Americans.

Identity statuses are not constant but situational. The relative privilege and stigma of different identities and attributes is relational and contextual. Thus, while African American status is often marginalized in a racially unequal society, its intersections with other dimensions of identity mean that it is not necessarily always marginal, or marginal in the same ways. Just as whiteness is not always privileging or always privileging in the same ways, the marked power of being black varies across different relationships with other racial categories and between one's blackness and one's other attributes, for example social class, gender, and native or immigrant status.

Globalization, Modernity, and the Multiply Influenced and Networked Character of Contemporary Identities

The situational and relational elements of identity are especially highlighted in a globalizing world where technology, migration, and the pace and movement of social life leave open many possibilities for multiple relations and environments. Gergen (1991) laments the frenetic state of the modern (or postmodern) self, where the individual is constantly assaulted by competing demands. He refers to this condition as *multiphrenia*, a state in which the self is almost constantly under siege and in which technology has amplified the number of demands that can be placed on the self simultaneously.

You are presumably familiar with the constant demands on our identities in daily life that Gergen discusses. Perhaps you are at lunch with a work colleague and an important text comes in from a family member. You quickly shift gears from your work role to your family role as you excuse yourself to give a brief response.

Instants later, you shift back to interacting with your work colleague, but with your family situation on your mind and dividing
your role commitments and attention. Then a workout partner
from your gym notices you in the café and interrupts you to discuss weekend plans. As you are talking, you get a phone call from
a friend in California sharing details about an upcoming wedding
you plan to fly out to in a few weeks. A local activist whom you've
met at climate change protests is putting up flyers at the café and
stops to chat you up and to encourage you to attend the next
demonstration. The demands on your self are coming in rapid
succession, your relations are scattered across time and space, and
so intense is the competition for your relational time that none of
the interchanges seems as deep or as effective as you would like
them to be. You are constantly at the mercy of these disparate and
competing calls.

Judith Howard (2000: 367–8) similarly discusses the modern
condition as one where the overwhelming pace of change and the
many networks in which people interact make identity dynamic,
multidimensional, and in a constant state of revision:

> At earlier historical moments, identity was not so much an issue;
> when societies were more stable, identity was to a great extent
> assigned, rather than selected or adopted. In current times, how-
> ever, the concept of identity carries the full weight of the need for a
> sense of who one is, together with an often overwhelming pace of
> change in surrounding social contexts—changes in the groups and
> networks in which people and their identities are embedded and in
> the societal structures and practices in which those networks are
> themselves embedded.

Concerns with identity and its complexities are perhaps not as
uniquely modern as Gergen and Howard suggest (see Jenkins
2014: 32), but the combination of increasing technological con-
nectivity and ever greater ability to shrink time and space between
social networks and identity commitments does amplify the multidimensional character of social life. As Mary Chayko (2017: 1)
argues, we are superconnected: "never in human history have so
many been connected to so many others, in so many ways, with
such wide-ranging social implications." This superconnectivity is,
of course, unequally distributed and not felt everywhere; thus in
much of southern Asia and sub-Saharan Africa computers, inter-

net access, and electricity are scarce (Chayko 2017: 1). But, where it is felt, its effect on identity is profound.

Technology connects us to online identities and facilitates our ability to manage multiple selves simultaneously. Online identities are rapidly mobile because they are not temporally restricted by the slower speed of physical bodies (even bodies aided by cars and planes) across different spaces. This mobility allows for a rapid "commuting" of identities, so that individuals can present different attributes of the self across various online platforms and communities. In an online context, identity becomes decentered and multiple (Turkle 1997). People can create separate, idealized personae across different online communities without reconciling them into a coherent whole (Turkle 1997; Davis 2011). Online platforms enhance the potential for selective self-presentation because their interfaces physically separate senders from receivers of information; they also allow actors to edit and revise this information easily, which gives them considerable control over their identity performances (Li and Tian, forthcoming). The potential for online technologies to increase the mobility and fluidity of multiple selves and to fragment the self into shifting, idealized presentations is notable. Yet online platforms also allow for identity strategies of integrating one's multidimensional attributes of self rather than "commuting" between them. José van Dijck (2013) found that platforms like Facebook and LinkedIn, rather than fragmenting the self, impose a degree of narrative uniformity and audience integration that does more to constrain segmented identities than to enable them. Mark Zuckerberg, the founder of Facebook, expresses the platform's underlying logic of identity integration in this form: "You have one identity. The days of you having a different image for your work friends or co-workers and for the other people you know are probably coming to an end pretty quickly" (quoted in Kirkpatrick 2011: 199; see also van Dijck 2013: 199). Instead of supplying a free-flowing environment for expressing separate identities to separate audiences, Facebook incentivizes people who, in physical space, are in the habit of segmenting audiences and identity attributes to integrate their many selves into one multifaceted self online. One's high school classmates, one's co-workers, one's family, one's political friends, one's worship friends, one's hobby friends, all those who interact with one's online identity become part of a multiply networked audience for the display of one's self.

Gergen's concern and similar perspectives on modern life's assault on the self imply that the complexities and divisions of modern living are threats to the stability and integrity of this self. A rapid and multidimensional social life pulls it in so many directions that its anchored core is lost. But the assumption that the social is the enemy of the personal self, its deconstructor or destroyer, fails to account for the notion that the social is the primary builder of the self. Modern life does embed us in multiple social networks across time and space, with divided commitments, and connects us to an ever greater diversity of relationships, social networks, and experiences, but these do not necessarily destabilize the self so much as allow us fresh opportunities to shape our identity (see Gubrium and Holstein 2000). The sources and the destiny of the self arise from the very social world that critics perceive as perilously challenging it (Gubrium and Holstein 2000: 100). These opportunities are subject to the power of institutions, social contexts, and our relations with others, but the multiple influences that pervade modern life also provide the creative material for personal and collective identities.

Erickson (2003) has demonstrated that diversity or variety in the types of people who form one's social networks presents advantages on a broad spectrum: for employment, for health, for cultural experience, and so on. Knowing more types of people exposes us to different kinds of experience and broadens our horizon. The experience of heterogeneity in social networks can add heterogeneity to one's social standpoint, one's web of affiliations, and one's attributes of identity salience, as well as to the numerous influences on one's worldview and sense of self. Much as a modern neighborhood changes when it becomes the home of new ethnic communities and starts to produce more subcultural enclaves and more spaces for cultural commerce and art, the modern self changes when it becomes shaped by a wider range of connections with different subcultures, different ethnic communities and their members, and people with different group affiliations. When Howard (2000) suggests that in past times identity was to a greater extent assigned rather than selected, she is addressing the ways in which an expansion of types of experiences leads to an expansion of potential identities. Gubrium and Holstein (2000: 101) link the multiple influences of self-construction to Mead and the classical roots of symbolic interaction when they note that, as "a malleable

structure that unfolds in the course of social interaction, the self
... [is] as varied as the relationships that mediate its formation."
The self is always a collaborative work in progress.

Goffman's interest in how the social self is managed, strate-
gized, and presented on the basis of audience and context further
reminds us that this self is an active work in progress on one's
identity. Like a well-written draft that has been revised many
times, the self takes on a narrative shape but is subject to change
and revision, additions and omissions. As Gubrium and Holstein
(2000: 101) put it,

> As we talk with ourselves or with others, we learn and inform each
> other about who we are and what we are. In a sense, we talk our
> selves into being. But not just anything goes. Social selves are not
> without design or restraint; they are not impromptu performances.
> What we say about ourselves and others is mediated by recogniz-
> able identities. We speak of ourselves in meaningful ways within the
> social contexts in which we communicate who we are. Selves do not
> just pop out of social interaction but are deftly assembled from rec-
> ognizable identities in some place, at some time, for some purpose.

The assembling of the self through combinations of attributes and
affiliations is an identity project made complicated by the demands
of modern life. Modern life embeds us in multiple social networks
across time and space, with divided commitments that complicate
our identity projects and add to the multidimensional character
of our identities. Interactionist theories of identity, and inequality or intersectionality theories of identity are brought together
in conceptions that view identity as a multidimensional resource,
deployed across a plurality of social contexts. Its fundamentally
social nature means that it is not only complex and multifaceted, much like modern social life and social networks themselves,
but also fluid and shifting in a multicontextual world. Chapter 5
explores how multidimensional identities are mobile across time
and space and deployed as shifting resources.

Further Reading

Crenshaw, Kimberlé. 1991. "Mapping the Margins: Intersectionality, Identity Politics, and Violence against Women of
Color." *Stanford Law Review* 43(6): 1241–99.

Crenshaw's foundational introduction to the concept of inter-sectionality challenges the notion that law responds neutrally. She demonstrates the multidimensionality of marginal subjects' lived experiences by examining the intersections of marginal-ized race, class, and gender identities among African American women.

Nash, Jennifer C. 2008. "Re-Thinking Intersectionality." *Feminist Review* 89(1): 1–15.
Both building upon and critiquing Crenshaw, Nash argues for expanding intersectional analysis beyond the multiply marginal-ized, so as to explore the fact that vectors of power and privilege are also intersectional and interact with vectors of marginality.

Brekhus, Wayne H. 1998. "A Sociology of the Unmarked: Redirecting Our Focus." *Sociological Theory* 16(1): 34–51.
In this useful companion to Nash's critique of intersectionality's lack of attention to privileging vectors, Brekhus argues that sociologists need to devote greater theoretical attention to the unmarked and to the normatively privileging aspects of identity. He highlights the advantages of understanding the relationship between privilege and marginality, including their intersections.

Bettie, Julie. 2014. *Women without Class: Girls, Race, and Identity*. Oakland: University of California Press.
In her ethnographic analysis of how Mexican American and white girls in a California high school perform class, subcul-ture, gender, and sexuality simultaneously, Bettie demonstrates the intersectionality of identities in interaction. Her book is an exemplar of modern intersectional analysis.

Wilkins, Amy C. 2008. *Wannabes, Goths, and Christians: The Boundaries of Sex, Style, and Status*. Chicago, IL: University of Chicago Press.
Wilkins ethnographically explores the identity projects of Puerto Rican "wannabes," goths, and evangelical Christians, demonstrating how young women in each subculture navigate the intersections of stigma and privilege to present identity and to negotiate their place in the social world.

Leap, Braden. 2017. "Survival Narratives: Constructing an Intersectional Masculinity through Stories of the Rural/Urban Divide." *Journal of Rural Studies* 55: 12–21.
Leap analyzes the intersections of race, class, gender, sexuality, and region in the narrative constructions of identity among

rural white men who define their intersectional rural masculinities through the oppositional construction of urban "danger" and difference.

Stroud, Angela. 2015. *Good Guys with Guns: The Appeal and Consequences of Concealed Carry*. Chapel Hill: University of North Carolina Press.

Stroud analyzes the symbolic boundary construction of mostly white middle-class men who define themselves as "good guys with guns." Sensitive to the privileging aspects of her research subjects' social locations, Stroud shows that their constructions of "goodness," masculinity, and identity are heavily tied to their socially unmarked positions.

Scott, Rebecca R. 2010. *Removing Mountains: Extracting Nature and Identity in the Appalachian Coalfields*. Minneapolis: University of Minnesota Press.

Another exemplar of modern intersectional analysis, Scott's study examines the roles that the intersections of gender, race, and class play in shaping people's sense of belonging to a region, as well as in shaping various constructions of that region. Scott shows how the intersecting classed, gendered, and raced representation of the region as a site of difference imagines it as an area suitable for environmental sacrifice.

Ribas, Vanesa. 2016. *On the Line: Slaughterhouse Lives and the Making of the New South*. Oakland: University of California Press.

Ribas worked for sixteen months in a slaughterhouse alongside Latina/o migrant and African American laborers in order to understand their work lives and identities in the New American South. She examines the incorporation experiences of Latina/o migrants and provides a complex picture of both racial identities and regional identity.

5

Mobility and Fluidity

The Omni-Contextual Nature of Identity

The fundamentally social nature of identity means that it is not only as complex and multifaceted as modern social life itself, but it is also fluid, mobile, and shifting in a multicontextual world. How do we use time and space to organize authenticity and multidimensionality? Identity is a multidimensional resource deployed across a plurality of social contexts. Multidimensional identities are mobile, and deployed as shifting resources across time and space, in the multifaceted social actor, in complex modern organizations, and in the meanings of places. As discussed previously, modern social life enmeshes people in numerous social networks, giving them a complex web of intersecting social standpoints and multifaceted relationships with others. Modern social actors can navigate this complexity by either bringing their many affiliations together simultaneously, to form one relatively enduring and multiply influenced social self that remains relatively constant across contexts (i.e. through identity multidimensionality), or they can balance their competing affiliations across time and space, regulating and shifting the salience of competing attributes and foregrounding and performing different selves across different sets of relationships and different social contexts (i.e. through identity mobility) (Brekhus 2015: 128). I use the concept of *identity mobility* to refer to the movement of identity across time and space. People move across different social contexts and deploy identities as portable resources that they activate or amplify in some settings and deactivate or tone down in others. Identity is not stationary or fixed but shifts with physical space and social location. Because multidimensionality is related to social standpoint and to social location, the metaphor of mobility also resonates with the ways in which people navigate their various intersecting and conflicting social positions of privilege and stigma. I also refer to identity fluidity to highlight that identity is in constant flux and changes across time and space. These metaphors are similar in that they both emphasize the transitory, migratory, and shifting character of social identities.

Michael Raphael (2017) argues for the dynamic, mobile character of the modern cognitivist self:

> While studies of identity go back millennia (concerning self, role, status, etc.), it is only recently that a plural cognitivist model is under development. In contrast to demographic representations, in the plural cognitivist model of the actor, social identity is not *just* [emphasis in the original] the mosaic of one's group memberships (race, class, gender, sexuality etc.), rather, who an actor is, phenomenologically, is dynamic within a range of possibilities of attribution . . . Identity corresponds to the ontology of the moment *relative* [emphasis in the original] to the locality of the social situation . . . This means integrating the role of identity in organizing experience (as observed over the course of a qualitative analysis) with how identity formation results from the "formal" multidimensionality of marked categories (race, class, gender, sexuality etc.) typically examined under the notion of "intersectionality."

In the pluralistic cognitivist model of identity, intersectionality and multidimensionality are integrated with cognitive sociological and intersectional approaches designed to examine how the competing attributes of stigma and privilege are narrated, negotiated, and presented across different social contexts. The pluralism of attributes and the range of different identity settings available to social actors and groups mean that the latter can develop these attributes differentially across a variety of contexts (Brekhus and Ignatow 2019: 9). What is stigmatized in one place can be highly socially valued and considered a source of pride in another (Raphael 2017).

Because we operate in multiple social worlds, where social value and sociocognitive markedness and unmarkedness are not cultural universals but context-dependent features of social life, our identities are fluid and subject to modification and renegotiation across different spaces and different times.

In his ethnographic study of gang-associated Latino youths in a southern California city, Victor Rios (2017) illustrates the importance of recognizing that people organize multidimensional facets of the self in a mobile way, presenting multiple identities across multiple settings. Critical of ethnographers who provide sensationalist one-dimensional accounts of "ghetto denizens" or "gangbangers" as a master status, Rios shows that authorities often see gang-associated youths as fixed types of people rather than as multifaceted actors dynamically shifting scenes and responding to changing environments and to different actors. While authorities often take complexity for granted in less marginalized people, the hypercriminalization of gang-associated Latino youths often robs them socially of the right to be seen as more than their presumed gang identity. Rios (2017: 9) argues that authorities and researchers alike too often view Latino youths from limited vantage points, as though they were looking at still photographs, frozen in time. They should see them instead through a video camera, striving to capture the motion as youths navigate multiple personae across different settings and interact with different institutions. By shadowing youths in this way, Rios discovered that, while they could play up tough gang personae, especially in response to agents of social control who expected them to adopt that role, they engaged in multiple performances as friends, students, regulars outside a store, and spent relatively little time behaving in the fixed ways that police, parole officers, and many school administrators and teachers imagined them to do. At the store where they congregated, the store's middle-aged South Asian American owner treated them as complicated multidimensional human beings, whom he defined more by their being kids and family members of loyal customers than by their gang-associated identities; they reciprocated for being seen in their full complexity by demonstrating care and empathy for his property and his customers (Rios 2017: 59). Recognizing that gang-associated youths navigate multidimensional selves in their fluid presentations of who they are across settings, Rios emphasizes the importance of authorities and policymakers avoiding one-dimensional and static views of complex, multidimensional people.

Identity Mobility: Identity Currencies and Identity Contexts

The *identity currencies* (the cultural resources we use to authenticate our identities) and the forms of cultural capital that we deploy to enact identity vary across different contexts. Much like in the case of monetary currencies, the exchange rate for identity currencies and the degree to which a currency will be recognized and valued or dismissed vary from setting to setting. "Native" identity currencies or cultural competencies are easily exchanged for social rewards and often taken for granted, while unusual, "foreign" identity currencies are called into question and require more complex interactional transactions to establish their social value. Individuals can draw upon context and upon specific forms of cultural capital, which are valued identity currencies in some settings and have been devalued in other settings. Individuals can shift or *code-switch* to different kinds of cultural capital and identity currencies across different environments, and this affords them the ability to move across and between different presentations of identity. Although the concept of cultural capital (Bourdieu 1984) has traditionally been applied to the most generally and widely valued forms of capital, such as upper-class cultural capital or dominant forms of cultural capital, there are also contextual, subcultural, and temporal and spatial forms of cultural capital that are specific to given spaces and contexts. Individuals can code-switch in and out of dominant and alternative forms of cultural capital. Carter (2003), for example, looks at *black cultural capital* and at more "generic" (majority white-dominant) *cultural capital* as two different linguistic and identity currencies that black individuals can deploy to navigate two competing social worlds. David Grazian (2003) examines *nocturnal capital* as a particular, leisure and urban nightlife-based form of identity capital that some individuals are able to deploy to enhance their status and their temporary identity authenticity claims in select cosmopolitan urban environs. Brekhus (2003, 2015: 111–46) examines the fluidity of identity attributes across settings, analyzing how individuals "commute" to specific spaces to amplify particular attributes, while downplaying others. Sociologists are increasingly interested in looking at the strategic presentation of identities across contexts as a form of cultural currency.

Carter (2003: 138–9) distinguishes between *non-dominant* and *dominant cultural capital*. Cultural capital provides us with the ability to "walk the walk" and "talk the talk" of the cultural power brokers in our society (Carter 2003: 138). Non-dominant cultural capital, then, consists of those resources that allow us to gain the favor of oppositional, subcultural, or minority cultural brokers and to gain "authentic" cultural status positions within these communities. One of the most evident instrumental uses of non-dominant cultural capital, Carter argues, is to navigate the complicated terrain of ethnic authenticity. As groups construct authenticity, they negotiate in-group cultural codes, expectations, and signals that convey cultural insider status.

The terrain of ethnic authenticity that I explored previously, in chapter 3, expands its boundaries as individuals bring their ethnicity and race into multiple contexts. Performances of one's identity are not the same on every social stage. Carter found, for example, that many African American youths consciously worked to embody both dominant and non-dominant cultural capital and strategically navigated these resources between family, peer, community, social, and legal spaces. Instrumentally, they employed their black cultural capital to "buy" themselves membership of and belonging into a group above and beyond what ascribed traits alone could give them, and they used dominant cultural capital to "buy" themselves employment and educational opportunities (Carter 2003: 140). Important in Carter's analysis is the way in which currencies flow across time and space, so that identity is not static and universal but context-dependent.

Kerry Rockquemore and David Brunsma (2002) show that, for some people, racial identity is protean, fluid, and entirely dependent on their specific social context. In analyzing their interviews with biracial individuals, they distinguish between those who integrate their mixed heritage into a "border identity," that is, a unified biracial identity with border identifiers, those who identify singularly with one side of their heritage (e.g. black), creating a "singular identity" with singular identifiers, and those who move between racial identities across different contexts, displaying a "protean identity." As the two researchers explain,

> instead of identifying as biracial, black, or white *consistently*, the individual will sometimes identify as black, at other times as white,

and still other times as biracial. The identity that is called up as representing the self is dependent solely on the individual's assessment of what is appropriate or *desirable in any given social setting*. Unique to this identity strategy is the ability to be accepted as an in-group member by different groups, which requires a complex mastery of various cultural norms and values and an ongoing awareness and monitoring of the presentation of self. (Rockquemore and Brunsma 2002: 69; emphasis added)

The complex mastery of navigating three collective racial identities through the deployment of proper cultural codes in each setting demonstrates a kind of nimbleness and flexibility in social situations. Just like being bilingual or multilingual, such switching of cultural codes requires multiple bases of cultural knowledge that not everyone has the skill to access. Protean respondents discussed their multiple cultural competencies and explained that having access to different social relationships and environments assisted them in developing different cultural codes for different settings. These individuals moved between cultural codes and switched with ease from standard to black vernacular English and from stiff body postures to loose, relaxed demeanors (Rockquemore and Brunsma 2002: 98).

The concept of *code-switching*, adapted to the presentation of identity, is a useful one for interpreting identity mobility. Originally developed in linguistics to refer specifically to language alternation, a process in which people move back and forth between different dialects and languages, code-switching is often referenced in sociology with respect to the linguistic and cultural practice that some African Americans engage in when they alternate between black vernacular and standard English. We can also think of the concept of social code-switching more broadly, as one of switching the cultural and linguistic currency one uses to match one's environment, turning them on and off and adapting to them. We can speak of code-switching one's body language as well as one's spoken language, and of altering one's cultural codes as well as one's speech codes. Language is, of course, one of the most significant cultural codes for authenticating one's identity. Multilingual fluency, like the multicultural fluency of racial proteans, allows one to more easily blend into multiple identities. The comedian Trevor Noah (2016: 56) makes this point when he explains in his autobiography that many incidents in his life convinced him that

> language, even more than color, defines who you are to people. I became a chameleon. My color didn't change, but I could change your perception of my color. If you spoke to me in Zulu, I replied to you in Zulu. If you spoke to me in Tswana, I replied to you in Tswana. Maybe I didn't look like you, but if I spoke like you, I was you.

Arguing for the power of linguistic code-switching to alter perceptions and metaphorically change one's colors to blend in to any environment, Noah describes himself as a "chameleon" who can deploy multilingual competencies in order to blend in and acquire insider status in many disparate groups.

Identity Commuting: Chameleons, Nocturnal Selves, and Micro-Temporal Identity Movements

The metaphor of the chameleon is one that appears in discussions of identity. Noah's statement "I could change your perception of my color" captures nicely how the strategic presentation of the self is designed to demonstrate that one's "true colors" are mutable and that changing them is contingent upon how an audience perceives them on the basis of the identity performance deployed before its eyes. Rockquemore and Brunsma's protean respondents, who moved between black, white, and biracial identities, accomplished changing their "racial colors" in a similar way: not by changing their skin color, but by altering audience perceptions about their race. They, too, were chameleons: "protean respondents describe themselves as moving in and out of differing social contexts, acting as chameleons who change their identities as quickly and as often as others change their clothes. They are neither compromised nor ashamed of their 'shifty' ways and find themselves validated at every turn" (Rockquemore and Brunsma 2002: 70–1). The chameleon is able to change colors across contexts in a small amount of time. The metaphor of the chameleon reflects both the relatively short duration of one's interactional shifts in identity and the central importance of one's environment to the colors, "true" or otherwise, displayed and perceived.

Being able to change one's identity as often as one's clothes suggests that identity shifts may occur as often as several times a day. We change clothes when we go to work, when we get back home from work, when we go out to the club, when we visit a friend. Both changing how we present our fashion through clothing and changing how we present our identities through appearance are processes related to where we are going and whom we will interact with. A gay suburban man in the 1990s who blended in as heterosexual during the day and came out as gay during the night explains: "What do [gays] wear outside the bar? Anything from a business suit to overalls on a tractor. Anything. Gay people are *chameleons*; we adapt into the scenery by day and like peacocks we come out with our true colors at night" (Brekhus 2003: 65; emphasis added). Because several suburban gay men I ethnographically interviewed in the 1990s presented heterosexual identities in the day in their New Jersey neighborhoods, but drove or rode public transportation to New York City at night or on the weekends to do their gay identities, I developed the concept of *identity commuters*. The distances and means of travel they used to get to New York to activate their gay identities resembled the occupational or work-related commuting of suburbanites; these people were in essence commuting to do "identity work." Recognizing daily temporal shifts in identity and the ways in which people use space and time to organize aspects of their selves and to segment or integrate their social networks helps us to further understand the socially constructed nature of identity. It is not just that identities can change historically, cross-culturally, or during the life course; they can change even in the course of a day. The protean, fluid nature of identities, as people use different currencies for them in different networks, complicates the matter.

People commute to identities for different reasons. Individuals with stigmatizing attributes that can be hidden may choose to conceal these negatively marked aspects in most environments, revealing them primarily only in the presence of others who share their marked identity. Marked identity enclaves such as ethnic neighborhoods (e.g. Little Italy, Chinatown) and gay enclaves (e.g. the Castro, Boystown) serve as destinations for commuters, travelers, and migrants to an identity. In contrast to the muting and diluting effects that ethnically and sexually unmarked spaces have on minority identities, marked enclaves serve as amplifying spaces for presenting and asserting one's pride in one's socially marked identity attributes (Brekhus 2003: 26). While unmarked groups and dominant institutions oppress, stigmatize, and exercise harsh social control over marked communities in most spaces, the enclave can serve as a mecca for self-expression, cultural pride, and identity politics organization.

Commuting between social networks to do different kinds of identity work in separate identity work environments is another style of exercising identity mobility. Protean racial individuals, who present themselves as white in white peer groups and settings and black in black peer groups and settings, are responding to relative racial advantage and relative racial stigma by adapting their identities to match their setting and placing a primary emphasis on belonging within and navigating separate peer groups. While still tied to the power of social groups to privilege or oppress, this form of traveling between different identities is a little different from the person's traveling to the enclave to escape oppression and to express his or her "true colors." For the protean, each racial identity is experienced as equally real. The identity commuter who engages in impression management to flow between separate social networks and different identity environments may, as racial proteans put it, feel "validated at every turn."

In addition to using space and social networks to organize their identities, commuters also use time. Individuals with marked social identities that they only activate or amplify some of the time will often bracket their amplified socially marked selves from their more mainstream everyday selves, using marked times such as the night and the weekend, in coordination with marked identity spaces, to segment their identities. Subcultural youths, for example, are especially likely to amplify their identities at night and on weekends. Although some punks, metal fans, and goths always present their identities in an amplified form, many do so only during the most identity-amplified periods. The night is a frontier that welcomes a greater range of presentations and attracts to the city temporal migrants who wish to escape the strictures and oppressions of everyday living (Melbin 1987; Brekhus 2003: 145). The connection between using space and time to escape to the city at night and expressing one's brighter colors to throw off the chains of oppressive, uniform, generic, unmarked, vanilla suburbia is often conveyed in subcultural genres committed to spaces and times of nonconformity. The hard rock–heavy metal band Rush, for example, has an identity commuter anthem entitled "Subdivisions," which portrays suburbs as sprawling, soulless, mass-produced generic spaces that stamp out deviance and creativity and provoke nighttime escape to the city (see https://www.lyrics.com/lyric/1819634/Rush/Subdivisions):

> Nowhere is the dreamer or the misfit so alone. Subdivisions ... Conform or be cast out ... But the suburbs have no charms to soothe the restless dreams of youth. Drawn like moths we drift into the city, the timeless old attraction, cruising for the action, lit up like a firefly just to feel the living night ...

Rush's portrayal, while overplaying the uniformity of suburbs, captures the importance of the city and of nighttime to people who want to find a place to escape in order to "light up" and amplify identities other than those mandated by the strictures of conformity, in which one has to lead a bland, unmarked, "nonthreatening" existence. Escaping to the city at night, the dreamer and the misfit alike can find space to express those parts of their self that daily living in suburban subdivisions, where even the houses conform, stamps out. The portrayal of suburbs as mass-produced and generic also suggests that authenticity is to be found in the more creative spaces of the city. While commuters are often associated with inauthenticity by subcultural insiders on account of the limited time they spend doing the identity, the emphasis in the Rush anthem is on cities as spaces of authenticity that can validate those travelers whose everyday existence is otherwise trapped in inauthentic, mass-produced, generic spaces.

The deployment of the night and urban spaces to do identity is not practiced just by individuals with marked identities. David Grazian (2003) documents how patrons of Chicago blues clubs adopt a *nocturnal self*, using the night and spaces associated with subcultural authenticity (e.g. "authentic" blues clubs, "authentic" dive bars) to perform alternative personae and to consume and practice distinct identities, different from their diurnal selves. Grazian (2003: 21) observes that individuals use their ability to appear subculturally versed and authentic and to navigate diverse spaces as savvy, urbanely hip, cosmopolitan sophisticates as *nocturnal capital*—a temporal type of cultural capital that offers status in urban spaces at night. Grazian (2008) further explores the performance of nocturnal selves in his study of college students navigating adult, cosmopolitanite, and heterosexually amplified identities in Philadelphia nightlife. Urban nightlife spaces are organized for consumption of recreational identities, masquerade, and play, and this makes them central locations for trying on, amplifying, or performing different identities and attributes of the self (Brekhus 2015: 138–9). They provide a space for people with marked identities to "come out" and visibly perform those identities, as well as a space for people with unmarked identities to complicate their identities by acquiring diverse kinds of nocturnal capital or to perform their unmarked identities in a more conspicuous and amplified way. Wealthy cosmopolitanites can perform their class identity through conspicuous dining at high-end restaurants, and young heterosexuals can perform their heterosexuality in amplified or identity-concentrated ways. Grazian (2008) shows, for example, that young heterosexual men travel together and congregate in the identity-amplifying spaces of urban nightlife to strategically perform, amplify, and display a heterosexual spirit to other men as a way to gain masculine currency among their peers; their display is consciously amplified in the homosocial context of congregating to do gender together, collectively, at night, as compared to their more moderate displays of heterosexuality in the day. Public urban nightlife spaces provide "the opportunity to perform a nocturnal self for an audience of anonymous strangers . . . where nocturnal roles can be rehearsed, social skills practiced, self-confidence tested" (Grazian 2008: 24) and forms of culturally specific identity capital can be learned and acquired.

Because urban nightlife is associated with leisure, consumption, and experimentation, it raises the issue of *identity play*. Herminia Ibarra and Jennifer Petriglieri (2010) argue that conceptions of identity as playful or experimental are missing from research on "identity work" and that the role of identity play in identity construction and management is neglected. They define identity play as "people's engagement in provisional but active trial of possible future selves" and distinguish it from identity work which seeks the "preservation of existing identities or compliance with externally imposed image requirements" (Ibarra and Petriglieri 2010: 13–14). The key difference between identity work and identity play is that play is concerned with potentially inventing and reinventing oneself, while work is concerned with maintaining one's already embraced, existing construction. While full-time "identity workers" with sometimes long-established identity careers that demonstrate their commitment to the identity are dismissive of "tourists," "wannabes," and people who "play" at the identity, play is no less analytically significant or serious than identity work. As Ibarra and Petriglieri (2010: 10) argue, playing at an identity is still serious business, because "we play with things that matter."

Considering identity play to be a strategy of trying on parts of our self, or refashioning elements of our multidimensional selves, or discovering new ways to balance our competing marked and unmarked attributes, one can observe that the framing of identity play in specific times and places allows one to "try on" identities temporarily, for possible future incorporation into the full-time self. The temporal and spatial bracketing of part-time selves allows for a cognitive distance between one's everyday self and other selves that one is trying on.

Temporal and Spatial Bracketing

Individuals who commute to do identity often use time and space to *bracket* different selves. Constructing a nocturnal self in the realm of nighttime consumption, leisure, and trying on identities separates the temporally marked nocturnal self as an entity distinct from the unmarked everyday (diurnal) self. Commuting to the city to amplify ethnicity or sexuality brackets one's culturally immersed ethnic or sexual self from one's "culturally diluted" everyday ethnic or sexual persona. Christena Nippert-Eng (1996) analyzes how the physical commute between home and work is accompanied by a corresponding "mental commute," which is signalled with transitional behaviors such as changing one's clothes and appearance and prepping for the transition from one's home to one's work self, then back again from the work to the home self. She refers to "mental bridges"—cognitive bridges we cross to shift from one identity to the next—arguing that extreme segmenters of work and home construct the equivalent of large bridges, like the Verrazzano-Narrows Bridge between New York and Staten Island or the Golden Gate bridge in San Francisco, while others construct relatively small bridge crossings (Nippert-Eng 1996: 108–9). Extreme segmenters with large bridges limit the number of mental crossings by limiting cross-realm phone calls, staying late at the office rather than finishing up work at home, avoiding inviting co-workers to their homes, and keeping work-related social networks separate from social networks related to leisure, neighbors, or non-work friends. While commutes sometimes involve actual physical bridges (as when "tunnel and bridge gays" take the bridge into New York), the metaphorical bridge that separates an everyday self who displays dominant cultural capital markers from a spatially and temporally bounded self who displays alternative forms of cultural or subcultural capital is instructive as to the cognitive aspects of identity construction. Traveling across space provides the instrumental benefits of ensuring that the likelihood of two different worlds colliding is lower; but it also provides a distance that makes it easier to symbolically mark off socially contextual selves as spatial, temporal, and network-specific presentations of who one is.

An even more temporally and spatially segmented example of transitory part-time identities is that of "vacation selves." Karen Stein (2019) analyzes the relationship between vacations and identity, suggesting that the power of vacations in shaping how people see themselves is evident in the fact that one can pilgrimage to the Sturgis Motorcycle Rally to become a full-fledged biker whether or not one is a biker during the rest of the year, or one can amplify an identity by going on a "mancation," complete with male-bonding extreme sports, poker, and golf, or to a "momcation," where mothers leave behind their children and husbands to spend time relaxing and talking among themselves. Stein examines three kinds of vacations—relaxation vacations, enrichment vacations, and staycations—and their influence on identities and identity strategies. Vacations, she argues, provide expanded opportunities for identity experimentation and play, as well as opportunities to do identity work. Stein (2019: 14) highlights vacations as a key site for identity shifts, arguing that such shifts

> encompass a new set of roles that a situation presents. They are a reflexive expression of internalized roles not expressed within the course of everyday life. In identity shifts people are not just adding new roles that are temporarily accessible; they are also playing with, or working with, existing identities by strategically emphasizing and deemphasizing and by strengthening and weakening them. They are building and changing or adding and subtracting.

Stein emphasizes that relaxation vacations often involve identity shifts that are playful interludes from mundane day-to-day responsibilities. This playfulness can also be used to bracket vacation as a frame where what one toys with for a limited period does not necessarily reflect everyday life and does not necessarily continue into it. Some vacation destinations even encourage bracketing, as in Las Vegas's conscious self-branding: "what happens in Vegas, stays in Vegas." One can be free to experiment with one's playful, "sinful" side in Sin City without taking a sinner identity back home. Relaxation vacationers engage in forms of identity play such as seeking adventure, taking risks, or inviting romance, all for the sake of acting out or trying on new or desirable roles (Stein 2019: 53).

By comparison, enrichment and edification vacationers engage in more conscious kinds of identity work in order to expand or enrich themselves by acquiring valued forms of cultural or subcultural capital. They often go to places where they develop a skill, or practice a hobby that engages their interests and relates to parts of themselves they want to develop further. These travelers collect cultural capital through their particular knowledges, their unusual experiences, their exotic destinations, and the relative inaccessibility of some of the destinations they travel to and activities they engage in (Stein 2019: 66). Just as some urban nightlife commuters develop a nocturnal self designed to convey a sophisticated cosmopolitan ability to move fluidly through and interact fluently within subcultural spaces, "artful travelers" are committed to an authentic "traveler self" that is distinct from a "tourist" identity. The following passage reflects how the artful traveler uses his or her ability to negotiate alternative forms of cultural capital and to claim an authenticity that distinguishes this person from inauthentic "tourists":

> While this is his first trip to China, it is not his first trip abroad. He has traveled to many European countries. Randal does not consider himself a "tourist." He frowns at the term, knowing he is something different. Tourists are the people on tour buses. The ones who follow tour guides and wear matching shirts so they do not split up and get lost. Randal knows himself to be more savvy than that and much more experienced with getting around the world. His background knowledge of China also differentiates him from the others. On a trip to the museum he does everything he can to leave behind

> his tour group and make the excursion his own. He tries to ask the
> guide questions in Mandarin. He disappears for half an hour and
> is spotted chatting with a group of young Chinese women work-
> ing as docents at the museum. He skips the group meal at a nearby
> restaurant that offers an English version of the menu and buys some
> dumplings and kabobs from a street vendor. (Stein 2019: 53)

In contrast to people who regard a stable, rooted identity as
authentic, the traveler fashions a multifaceted mobile self whose
authenticity is dependent on being able to move fluidly through
the world, deploying various forms of multicultural capital in
order to integrate him- or herself into multiple settings. Travel is
not just a chance to experience the world, it is an opportunity to
self-fashion through a worldly performance that shows that one is
adventurous, open-minded, and adaptable (Stein 2019: 80).

The movement to and navigation of places that both identity commuters and identity travelers engage with reflects the
importance of place to the organization and formation of social
identities. People use place to accentuate and develop their identities and to enmesh themselves in social networks and settings
where they can deploy various kinds of cultural capital so as to
demonstrate their authenticity to one another. Access to different
identity destinations is not equally distributed, and even places
that welcome people with marked identity attributes do not welcome all the members of marked groups with the same openness.
Place is important to shifts in identity both at the micro level of
daily commutes and at the more global and longer-term level of
extended vacations. It is also significant for the shifts in identity
that people experience when moving from one environment to
another.

Identity Mobility and Place: Local Identity Cultures and How Places Make Us and How We Make Places

A petite, tattooed woman in her early thirties with an Ivy League
degree moves from Boston, Massachusetts to Portland, Maine. She
is surprised how the move changes her very sense of self; after years
of representing herself as a lesbian without giving much thought
to the kind of lesbian she might be, she begins to define herself

as a "stone butch" (see Brown-Saracino 2018: 1). Her social networks and the basis on which she forged them also change; she co-founds a meetup group for butch individuals and approaches her friendship networks and self-identification in a very different way in Portland from how she did in Boston (Brown-Saracino 2018: 1). Similarly, another woman moved from Northampton to Ithaca and discovered that while she lived in Northampton she thought of herself as "lesbian" or "butch," but her identity has since shifted and while she still lives with her woman partner, she increasingly identifies as a carpenter and a gardener and "wonders when 'lesbian' stopped being the defining facet of her self and how she came to spend evenings beside working-class men in a heterosexual bar" (Brown-Saracino 2018: 3). Each of these cities has different *sexual identity cultures* that shape how people organize and define their own identities (Brown-Saracino 2018).

Japonica Brown-Saracino (2018: 4) develops the concept of sexual identity cultures as entities (1) distinct from the broad, diffuse, city-spanning or even international "leather" or "bear" subcultures (two self-identified subcultures formed around sexual styles) that Hennen (2008) identifies as sexual cultures, yet (2) larger than something like the *idioculture* of a little league baseball team (see Fine 1979). In other words, sexual identity cultures are local cultures created by specific city ecologies and identity climates. Brown-Saracino presents four such cultures in four small US cities as a case study of the more general issue of *local identity cultures*. Even in an age of globalization and corporatization, she argues, places maintain distinctive personalities because, in addition to being social, we are fundamentally local creatures, deeply shaped by our most immediate regional surroundings and interactions. Thus it is likely that "the way one 'does' professor, doctor, plumber, or stay-at-home-mom is different in Santa Fe than in Denver, and that what it feels like to be single or married varies between Tampa and Tallahassee" (Brown-Saracino 2018: 6). Our basic notions of identity and difference are shaped by the city in which we live (Brown-Saracino 2018: 3).

Brown-Saracino highlights the degree to which self-understanding and group understanding are collective accomplishments; and she does so by examining very small and local cultures of sexual identity. Local cultures and place-based elements have a substantial effect on the presentation of collective elements of identity.

Lesbian, bisexual, and queer (LBQ) identities vary substantially across the cities under study, while being relatively coherent within each city. In Ithaca, New York, LBQ women lived as identity integrators of a post-identity politics. That is, they lived in an ambient community with a sense of belonging that was based on a number of voluntary ties with a diverse network of people with whom they shared some identity attributes such as profession and age; but they were not in a specific lesbian subculture or enclave and largely identified as multifaceted people rather than presenting their sexual identity as a central facet of the self. In San Luis Obispo, California, residents embraced identity politics, identified as lesbians, and framed sexual identity as an essential and defining element of the self. In Portland, Maine, residents defined themselves using hybrid, hyphenated queer identities. They broke queer (LBQ) identities down into hybrid, particularized, specific identities such as "queer punk", "stone butch," "high femme," "queer dyke," "trans butch," or "gender queer." Finally, in Greenfield, Massachusetts there was a split between lesbian–feminist long-timers and post-identity politics newcomers. Brown-Saracino (2018: 198) argues that the differences between the sexual identities of the LBQ women in these cities are explained by three general characteristics: (1) abundance and acceptance (the number of LBQ residents who live in the area in proportion to the population and how they are residentially dispersed across the area), (2) place narratives (the narrative story the city tells about what it is; the city's statement of its place identity), and (3) the city's socioscape (residents' perspectives on the social, cultural, and demographic traits of residents, especially LBQ ones). Residents learned about the local socioscape through the stories other residents told and through their own interactions with other residents; for example, when a newcomer to San Luis Obispo argued that socialization shapes gender and sexuality and the rest of the women around her gently disagreed, arguing that sexual identity is rooted in biology, the newcomer abandoned her position and began to reinterpret the matter through the lens of local LBQ standards for identity worldview (Brown-Saracino 2018: 218). Socioscapes provide local auxiliary characteristic standards and forms of collective community cultural capital that vary across different cities. In consequence, identities, LBQ and other, are mobile and fluid across cities with different place narratives and socioscapes. Identities are multifaceted, and their multidimensional features are activated in different ways as one moves across and to different settings. Who one is in San Luis Obispo and who one is in Ithaca are not the same thing, because both a space and the narrative cultures of the people in it shape individual narratives and perceptions of self.

Ashleigh McKinzie (2017) observes how the local cultures and historical, sociopolitical and geographic contexts of two small US cities with different local histories—Joplin in Missouri and Tuscaloosa in Alabama—lead to different configurations of social inequalities and senses of community and identity with respect to the race, age, gender, and class of tornado victims. Although McKinzie uses different conceptual terms from those of Brown-Saracino, her analysis of the community-specific effects on perceptions of disaster recovery, as they relate to the intersections of race, class, and gender in each city, demonstrates similar insights about the importance of place in shaping identities, narratives, and the consequences of identity. McKinzie conducted three years of fieldwork that included 162 interviews and the use of archival data to explore how sociohistoric contexts influenced perceptions of long-term disaster recovery from tornadoes and how perceptions of recovery vary within and across social groups and geographic contexts. In particular, she focuses on how the two different cities varied in their perceptions of recovery especially with respect to intersectional identities and inequalities.

McKinzie (2017: 525) argues that places "are infused with meaning created by institutional forces, and consequently that meaning influences individual actions, attitudes, and identities"; hence the histories of both towns influence racialized and classed perceptions of disaster relief and recovery. She highlights the differing histories of the two communities. Joplin was a mining town and a "sundown town" that restricted the mobility of African Americans who wanted to live in the community or to appear there after sundown; its racial narrative is presented as a case of "nothing to see here," since the historical removal and exclusion of African Americans in the region is largely invisible to whites and community leaders. As a result of Joplin's more racially homogenous makeup (a homogeneity produced by its earlier history as a sundown town) whites there express a color-blind ideology. Tuscaloosa was a southern segregated city with a history of visible racism; it was ordered to desegregate in the 1950s. It is also a university town. Residents were more race-conscious. The histories of these cities shape the narratives that people tell about them and the intersectional identities of both the cities and their residents. Thus people's narratives about their city and its residents reproduced social inequalities in disaster recovery.

Demonstrating that the identity of cities fluctuates depending on which group of inhabitants narrates its identity, white residents in both cities narrated a long-term social leveling effect of the tornado and the subsequent disaster response, suggesting that the upheaval of a major disaster enduringly brought the city together as one community, across social boundaries of race and class. African American residents disputed the permanence of social leveling and instead saw their communities as being divided but coming together during an emergency, for a fleeting, micro-temporal moment. Whereas white residents regarded social leveling as a core element of their city's identity that the disaster brought out, black residents considered such leveling as a bracketed, temporary identity shift in the face of unusual circumstances. Leveling was not etched into the community's identity, it was a context-specific performance of the city's people under extraordinary conditions.

Applying Brown-Saracino's idea of the socioscape, the stories that residents told one another and others about their city, its identity, and the identity of its residents affected how they responded to issues of social inequality. Joplin's white residents narrated their community through a lens of color-blind racism. Because they had limited interracial interactions and confrontations, they narrated their city as a unique (and superior) community, better able to overcome a disaster than Tuscaloosa, on the grounds that Joplin has a "Midwestern work ethic" and Midwestern values such as not wanting handouts, and that its African American community is different from and better than other African American communities—which implicitly meant more middle class, Midwestern, and mainstream (McKinzie 2017: 529–30). They contrasted their Midwestern values and work ethic with those of the people in Tuscaloosa after their tornado and in New Orleans after Hurricane Katrina, whom they criticized for just waiting for help from the government. Their socioscape and ideology about the characteristics of Joplin and its residents (in contrast to residents of other cities like New Orleans) formed a narrative of community identity that simultaneously advanced the color-blind racist work of ignoring racially discriminatory policies and outcomes. White residents represented their city as a friendly Midwestern city without racial inequalities, and they did so by emphasizing its core Midwesternness and by cognitively and discursively assimilating its racial others into a uniform, unraced identity perception of the city. African American residents, however, challenged this white socioscape and the notion that it possessed special qualities of helpfulness and independence and uniquely positive Midwestern values. Black residents also challenged claims about Joplin's unique self-sufficiency, pointing out that Joplin appeared to receive a greater outpouring of state and federal relief (Tuscaloosa received $10.1 million in aid after its tornado, while Joplin received more than $150 million), as well as volunteers from other areas, all because it was a "white" community (McKinzie 2017: 530–1). In contrast to Joplin's white residents, those of Tuscaloosa, white and black alike, did not describe their recovery in terms of a set of city values; they focused instead on the lack of help from the government and on why they appeared to be forgotten by comparison to Joplin. For many Tuscaloosa residents, racial inequality has been a visible feature of community life and a part of its narrated history; and members of the community were more likely to consider these racialized dynamics as a part of the city's identity and as a reflection of its relative status when it came to receiving disaster recovery support.

Places both have identities and shape the identities of their travelers and their inhabitants. The identity of places affects how others perceive them; it also affects the distribution of resources to and from them. Comparing two studies of place, one focused on how it shapes LBQ identities and the other on how it shapes the racialized and classed dynamics of perceptions around community disaster recovery, we can see that the stories communities tell about themselves, about the kind of community they are and the kinds of people they have, encourage perceptions that shape how people see themselves and others around them. People's identities are tied to the contexts and the *narrative environments* (Gubrium 2005) in which they operate.

Community identities are fluid and contextual. These identities, collectively narratively constructed, vary across different social networks and across time and space. Joplin's identity as a Midwestern city "without much [inequality] to see" moves comfortably through most of its predominately white communities without being challenged or contested. The conservative, libertarian frame through which many of its white residents see themselves and their community fits comfortably with privileged, unmarked, color-blind racism. The city's identity is not static, however. When under the analytic scrutiny of many of its African American residents, this identity changes, and we see cohesion and unity becoming the temporary presentations of a city that responds to a crisis, but whose more enduring identity is as a place where inequalities exist and persist.

Identity and Time: Long-Term Identity Shifts, Migrations, and Transformations

Previously we examined identity commutes and short-term shifts in identity. In addition to these shifts across small moments of time, there are also long-term identity shifts and transformations. These processes occur both with individual identities and with collective ones. Examples of long and enduring individual identity shifts are personal awakenings, identity lifestyle changes, and autobiographical revisions. Examples of collective identity transformations include changes in the racial and ethnic identities of European immigrants such as Irish, Italian, and Jewish European, whose group identities in the United States have moved from being ethnic minorities to becoming basically white.

In her analysis of abstainers (people who abstain from a particular thing such as alcohol, drugs, sex, meat, or material consumption), Jamie Mullaney (2006) highlights the critical importance of duration to identity constructions. Duration matters with respect to both *when* an identity started (or ended) and *whether* the identity is regarded as temporary or permanent. Mullaney refers to four temporal types of abstainers: (1) waiters (people who have not previously engaged in the behavior and whose current abstinence is assumed to be temporary), (2) time-outers (people who have previously engaged in the behavior and whose current abstinence is assumed to be temporary), (3) nevers (people who have not previously engaged in the behavior and whose current abstinence is assumed to be permanent) and (4) quitters (people who have previously engaged in the behavior and whose current abstinence is assumed to be permanent) (Mullaney 2006: 84–5). Of these four durational types, time-outers and quitters are the most significant for studying identity shifts, as they represent the temporal distinction between people who commute to an identity and experiment with becoming permanent abstainers and people who make a more permanent transformative mental journey to become identity abstainers.

Thomas DeGloma and Erin Johnston (2019) analyze the role of *cognitive migrations* in narrative identity work. In contrast to the physical migration of an individual or group from one geographic community to another, a cognitive migration involves the mental movement of an individual or group from one social identity or worldview to another (DeGloma 2014: 148; DeGloma and Johnston 2019: 623). Cognitive migrations, conceived of as *identity migrations*, differ from identity commutes in that they entail a more permanent relocation of one's identity. One is no longer just "trying on" an identity, one is "living" it.

DeGloma (2014) provides a detailed analysis of a particular type of cognitive migration: that of the "awakener," whose self is temporally divided between what the person sees as an "unenlightened" or naïve past and an awakened present. Awakeners can experience various kinds of conversions or awakenings, be they religious, spiritual, or political; and they can be either converts or apostates. Such people use vocabularies of liminality to describe their passage or movement between two mutually exclusive cognitive standpoints or worldviews. They use the metaphorical language of mobility and migration to discuss their journey from a previous, false state of being to their new, true state of mind, and the language of authenticity to contrast their current, awakened, and true selves with their previous selves, false and inauthentic. DeGloma discusses two kinds of trajectories that people who experience an awakening use to narrate their change. In one, the individual moves to and experiences a new awakening and self-identity slowly and gradually, through a series of steps, as though walking up a staircase. In the other, the individual experiences identity mobility more dramatically as a radical shift in his or her self-understanding, as though riding an express elevator to this new self-understanding.

Individuals account for their significant changes of consciousness, mind, and identity, expressed as transformative experiences, powerful discoveries, and newly embraced selves or worldviews through autobiographical stories that have elements in common with the stories of others, who have experienced similar cognitive migrations (DeGloma and Johnston 2019). DeGloma and Johnston (2019: 625) argue:

> Cognitive migrations, as a form of self-change, are accomplished in, and sustained through, the act of storytelling. From this perspective, our selves become meaningful as characters in stories we tell, to ourselves and to others, about who we are, about how we have arrived at our current situations, and about our beliefs, aims, and objectives in the world.

When individuals embark upon cognitive migrations, they create and structure a narrative plot of their life course, so as to plant their allegiance to a particular sociomental community or collective in a pluralistic and complex social environment (DeGloma and Johnston 2019: 625). The narrative templates they use are not entirely their own; they borrow significantly from similar narratives of others, who are a part of their community (much as the residents of a physical community such as a city might share similar narratives about the local socioscape).

In addition to *awakenings*, DeGloma and Johnston identify two other styles of identity migration: the *self-actualization* and the *quest*. Self-actualizations, rather than narrating a radical break between a previous "false" consciousness and a new "true" consciousness, express discovering, accepting, or reaffirming a "true self" that was dormant, muted, unrealized, or hidden until it was discovered or rediscovered. These narratives bridge a past self and a present self as coherent parts of a temporally continuous trajectory that was hidden. They downplay differences between past and present worldviews through the "construction of an underlying true self" that they came to realize through their exposure to a community and its associated worldview (DeGloma and Johnston 2019: 630). Questers reflect a particularly mobile and fluid self. They describe their migrations as an ongoing process and an endless string of continuous beginnings. One of Johnston's interviewees describes the questing approach to identity thus: "We have a direction, not a destination. We are going East, but you can't get East. You can only go East" (see DeGloma and Johnston 2019: 633). Questers are engaged in an ongoing process of identity construction and self-transformation that is always being revised and reshaped through new exposures and experiences.

Examining the ways in which people narrate the shifts in their identity reveals the potential for identities to change and be reshaped over time, as these people come into contact with new communities, changing social networks, and different cultural reference groups. Various life experiences and circumstances generate shifts in social identity. There are parallels between how individuals narrate and present their autobiographical identities and how collectives narrate the relations between their past and their present. To illustrate this, let us consider how people construct their identities at high school reunions and the parallels between this process and how nations construct their present identities in relation to the past.

Vered Vinitzky-Seroussi analyzes identity presentation at high school reunions, demonstrating that one issue individuals struggle with is how to show continuity between their situated identity in the reunion and their past with their high school peers. They often engage in reparative narrative work in order to maintain consistency, as their past is not always easily congruent with who they are today. Vinitzky-Seroussi (1998: 130) observes that "people attend . . . reunions ostensibly looking for changes," but that in fact they are primarily oriented toward overlooking and dismissing those changes, so as to focus on how "they and their [former] friends have stayed the same." Because of our cultural commitment to the idea of a stable core identity, we seek to narrate ourselves as "true" to a core that has not fundamentally altered over the years, even if it requires narrative work to bind the past and the present coherently. To bolster the conviction of a true self, reunion attendees dismiss visible changes as merely external appearances, not a threat to internal consistency (Vinitzky-Seroussi 1998: 131).

Narrative revision and repair to maintain continuity between past and present identities also occurs at the collective level. Barry Schwartz (1997) illustrates how Abraham Lincoln, as a historical figure and as a symbol of America's biography and national identity, has undergone changes in his public identity that are based upon when he was commemorated and who commemorated him. While Lincoln was opposed to racial equality and considered whites to be superior, his transformation into a symbol of racial equality and justice was accomplished through revisions of the nation's past identity that aimed to make it more consistent with its declared present values. Lincoln's identity shift from conservative symbol of the status quo to a champion of racial justice followed changes in the society as a whole. During the Jim Crow era in the 1920s, President Warren Harding and Chief Justice and former President William Howard Taft stood before a crowd of both Union and Confederate Army veterans during the dedication of the Lincoln Memorial and proclaimed the event as a restoration of the brotherly love between the North and the South; Harding had also stated that the supreme chapter in American history was union, not emancipation (Schwartz 1997: 469). Key to their commemoration was the idea that the Lincoln Memorial was a celebration of regional, not racial, reconciliation (Schwartz 1997: 469). This version of Lincoln was conservative and fit with a view of Lincoln as someone whose primary achievement was to save the union, emancipation being just a secondary means to that larger primary end. It was a view of Lincoln that fit well with the Jim Crow era of its time. Lincoln's public identity began to shift first during the New Deal and then during the Civil Rights era, so that modern commemorations of him are often tied to emphasizing racial equality, and even the elimination of poverty. As Schwartz (1997: 487) points out, Lincoln's aims in war were neither a multiracial inclusive union nor a poverty-free one; but modern commemorative apparatuses center on these values. Emphasizing how nations maintain a continuous identity in the face of identity shifts in their values, Schwartz (1997: 489–90) presents the following argument:

> Lincoln's changing image legitimates changing social realities by making them seem continuous with his values and intentions ... Applied to our predecessors, looking glass perceptions exaggerate consensus over time. It is hard for most Americans to imagine Abraham Lincoln referring to the slaves he emancipated as "niggers" or deliberately planning to ship them to other continents. It is easier to imagine his thinking of slaves as we do: ordinary men and women who have been wronged and must be welcomed into society as full citizens. It is easier to think this way of Lincoln because our sense of who we are as a nation presupposes a sense of who he was as a person.

In the context of a present society where the stated ideals, even if unrealized in practice, include racial equality, commemorative and narrative work must be done to bridge the present with the past and to make the national identity seem continuous and coherent even if significant change has occurred. Like the autobiographical identity work done at high school reunions to connect past selves to present selves, a nation's identity work will also attempt to reconcile the past in order to make it consistent with and meaningful in the present.

It should be noted here that, while identity is fluid, contingent, and continuously changing, the lengths that individuals and collectives go to to maintain a sense of stability to a true self, or to a true national character, suggest that identity is not a chaotically fluid free-for-all, with no sense of grounding or meaning. Postmodern theorists of identity have sometimes celebrated and sometimes problematized the fluidity of identity; it signalled to them the death knell of essentialist notions of identity as something rooted, central, and enduring. Although these theorists point, correctly, to the always moving and changing contours of identity, the ways in which individuals and communities make sense of shifting identities by finding consistency remind us that the relationship between fluidity and stability is a complicated one. We cannot entirely dismiss stability as a potential objective—and therefore as a feature—of identity even in a complex, multidimensional, ever-changing social reality.

Collective Ethnic and Racial Fluidity

Earlier in this chapter we explored how individuals can navigate fluid ethnic and racial identities. Their racial and ethnic statuses can increase or decrease in salience or change altogether across different settings. Just as life experiences can lead to shifts in self-identity, changes in social conditions at the aggregate level can affect the mobility and salience of collective identity attributes. Scholars interested in the shifting saliences of ethnic and racial identity boundaries and in the strength of racial and ethnic identities have noted, for instance, how intensified economic competition can lead to heightened racial and ethnic protests and to greater racial and ethnic identity salience (e.g. Olzak 1993). Moreover, just as individuals can respond to shifting environments and contexts by changing their racial and ethnic identities or the salience with which they deploy or downplay them, collectives can also shift their identities across spatial and temporal environments.

As an example of how this can happen, take the case of white European ethnic identities in the United States. Richard Alba (1990) analyzes survey research and interviews among European immigrants to the United States to argue that European ethnic immigrant identities in the United States have become increasingly diluted and are no longer connected to strongly ethnic structures. Significant ways in which white European ethnic groups differed with respect to occupational niche, residence in ethnic neighborhoods, and intermarriage have faded; only some vestiges of ethnic cultural practices remain, and these are often only intermittently salient in specific, family-based contexts. Collectively, white European ethnic identities have been transformed: from identities of relatively high-density and occupationally, residentially, and socially networked ethnic communities, they turned into more widely dispersed and diluted identities that are increasingly becoming nondescript and closer to a generic white.

Mary Waters (1990) similarly argues that what remains for most white European ethnics is *symbolic ethnicities* that are essentially leisure time activities, tied to nuclear family traditions and reinforced by the voluntary and enjoyable aspects of being ethnic, but that hold little cost. White ethnics today often live largely as generically white people and commute to ethnic identities for family occasions and leisure activities. Waters conducted field research among white people in the suburbs of Philadelphia, Pennsylvania and San Jose, California, finding that later-generation descendants from European countries maintained these symbolic ethnicities, doing strong ethnicity temporarily as leisure but not living in ethnic neighborhoods, not marrying co-ethnics, not joining organizations tied to their ethnicity, and not working in jobs associated with their ethnicity. For example, Irish Americans today will often amplify their ethnicity on St. Patrick's Day and identify as Irish on family holidays or vacations, but will not be heavily invested in Irish identity as a full-time, salient, visible aspect of their everyday reality. Waters argues that, for late-generation white European ethnics, ethnicity is a fluid and optional resource that only influences one's life if one wants it to. She notes, of course, that no-cost symbolic ethnicities in the United States are most available to white ethnic groups and far less available to African Americans, Latinas/os, Asian Americans, and American Indians. The shift in white ethnic identities manifested at the individual level, as a personal choice over the option to be ethnic or not, also reflects a corresponding change in the collective significance of white ethnic identities. Identities such as Italian American, Polish American, and Irish American have lost much of their ethnic potency, as the level of discrimination against these backgrounds has decreased over time. These groups have come to be seen more and more as "unhyphenated whites." Historically, ethnic immigrant groups from Ireland, Italy, and Poland were strongly ethnicized and had fewer options to integrate into a generic space, or to live as generic white Americans most of the time. Rather than travel to amplify symbolic ethnicities during certain times and spaces as "ethnic commuters," they lived a more enduringly accentuated ethnic identity, as "ethnic lifestylers." The salience of ethnicity for white ethnics has declined both for individuals and for collective groups as a whole.

Ashley Doane (1997) shows how dominant group ethnicity is dynamic and shifts over time. During intergroup resource competition, the relative advantages and disadvantages of asserting or masking specific group identities influence the shaping and mobility of the boundaries of those identities. The construction of the ethnic order of a society is a contested terrain, where core elements of dominant group identity, including the legitimacy of dominant status and the ability to appropriate national identity, are open to contestation, challenge, negotiation, revision, and redefinition (Doane 1997: 386). Doane traces the evolution of dominant ethnic identity in the United States in several stages. Colonists constructed an early dominant English settler identity, in opposition to that of American Indians and non-English immigrants. After independence, an Anglo-dominated "American" identity developed through group appropriation of a national identity that advanced through slow immigration, exclusion from citizenship of American Indians and African Americans, and the absorption of non-English colonial era immigrants. Since then, there has been a slow, gradual shift in dominant American identity, which has stretched to include greater numbers of groups of European ancestry (Doane 1997: 386). These changes reflect strategic adjustments to deploying identity as a resource used by the dominant group—and by other groups absorbed into it—in response to changing social conditions. Doane documents that a first stretching of dominant group boundaries was the assimilation and incorporation of immigrants of Northern and Western European Protestant ancestry. This process came in response to increases in immigration from Southern and Eastern Europe and to an accentuation of racial politics. The consequence was a dilution of English American ethnicity and a more expanded white Anglo-Saxon Protestant (WASP) American identity. A second expansion of dominant group boundaries has been happening since the 1960s, as Southern and Eastern European immigrant groups have gradually been incorporated into a general white European unmarked ethnic "American" identity. For the emergent European American unmarked ethnic group, the core identity is its distinction from non-European and non-white groups.

The movement of dominant ethnic identities is not always migration toward a broader accumulation of more ethnic attributes within the collective. The process of dominant group boundary change is uneven and can have moments of boundary retraction as well as expansion. Doane argues that the broadening of dominant group boundaries to include more white European ethnic attributes within the dominant group's collective ethnic identity came during a period of economic expansion that yielded more resources, which rendered the inclusion of subordinate groups and subordinate group mobility relatively cost-free. In the face of economic uncertainty, the dominant group may enforce and present a narrower range of ethnic attributes as being "authentically" American. Doane predicts that the forces that reduced the boundaries between European American groups (upward mobility, assimilative institutions, intermarriage, perceived threats from non-European groups) will lead to a continued consolidation of the European American (white American) identity and that, as a dominant ethnicity, this European American identity will become a "hidden ethnicity" whose character will be largely taken for granted as generically non-ethnic, except in ethnic contexts and ethnic conflicts. Further expansion of dominant group boundaries might create a slow drift toward a more multicultural identity, as diverse groups, for example Latina/o, become socially, politically, and economically more integrated; but Doane also warns that increasing intergroup antagonism and conflict that bolsters the building of walls around the current boundaries of dominant ethnic identity is also a significant possibility. How the dominant group defines itself and how it is defined by others will have a significant impact on the future of symbolic and material relations between groups (Doane 1997: 389).

Further Reading

Rios, Victor M. 2017. *Human Targets: Schools, Police, and the Criminalization of Latino Youth*. Chicago, IL: University of Chicago Press.

Rios ethnographically observes gang-associated Latino youths in southern California, demonstrating that they are multifaceted individuals who shift their identity presentations across different spaces and in relation to different actors. In contrast to ethnographies of urban youths that portray the latter as relatively fixed by their "marked identities" as gang members or "delinquents," Rios shows that gang-associated youths navigate multidimensional selves through their fluid presentations of the self across changing settings.

Rockquemore, Kerry, and David L. Brunsma. 2002. *Beyond Black: Biracial Identity in America*. Thousand Oaks, CA: SAGE.

Rockquemore and Brunsma explore the ways in which biracial individuals navigate their racial identities as "border identifiers" who integrate a unified biracial identity, "singular identifiers" who identify with one side of their heritage, or "proteans" who shift their racial identity fluidly across contexts, depending on the setting they are in.

Brekhus, Wayne H. 2003. *Peacocks, Chameleons, Centaurs: Gay Suburbia and the Grammar of Social Identity*. Chicago, IL: University of Chicago Press.

Brekhus analyzes how suburban gay men use space and time to negotiate their identities. He analyzes the mobility of identity in the nightly or weekly commutes to gay identity that suburban "gay commuters" make to New York City to activate and amplify their gay identities.

Grazian, David. 2003. *Blue Chicago: The Search for Authenticity in Urban Blues Clubs*. Chicago, IL: University of Chicago Press.

Grazian analyzes the mobile and fluid navigation of authenticity through the ways in which travelers to urban areas at night negotiate temporal "nocturnal selves" in pursuit of the night-time identity of an urbane and sophisticated cultural insider.

Ibarra, Herminia, and Jennifer L. Petriglieri. 2010. "Identity Work and Play." *Journal of Organizational Change Management* 23(1): 10–25.
Ibarra and Petriglieri introduce the concept of "identity play." They distinguish identity play from identity work. Identity play is engaged with the potential to invent or reinvent oneself, while identity work is focused on reinforcing one's already existing self.

Nippert-Eng, Christena E. 1996. *Home and Work: Negotiating Boundaries through Everyday Life.* Chicago, IL: University of Chicago Press.
Nippert-Eng analyzes how people navigate their home and work lives and identities, demonstrating that some individuals largely integrate the two, while others segment and commute between two very distinct bracketed roles and engage in rituals to maintain their separate work and home selves.

Stein, Karen. 2019. *Getting Away from It All: Vacations and Identity.* Philadelphia, PA: Temple University Press.
Stein offers a unique angle on identity mobility by analyzing vacation identities. She gives a detailed analysis of relaxation vacations, enrichment vacations, and staycations and the kinds of identity work and identity play that each type of vacation allows us to perform.

Brown-Saracino, Japonica. 2018. *How Places Make Us: Novel LBQ Identities in Four Small Cities.* Chicago, IL: University of Chicago Press.
Brown-Saracino analyzes the mobility of identities by demonstrating how places make us and shape our identities in very local ways. Demonstrating that LBQ individuals construct their identities and define themselves very differently depending on where they live, she makes the case for understanding the context-dependent nature of collective identities.

McKinzie, Ashleigh E. 2017. "A Tale of Two Cities: Variations in Perceptions of Disaster Recovery and the Importance of Intersectionality." *Sociology of Race and Ethnicity* 3(4): 522–37.
McKinzie observes how the identities of two small US cities disrupted by tornadoes (Joplin in Missouri and Tuscaloosa in

Alabama) fluctuate according to the group that narrates their identities. Collective identities of cities are fluid and shifting depending on events and on which groups narrate these identities.

DeGloma, Thomas, and Erin F. Johnston. 2019. "Cognitive Migrations: A Cultural and Cognitive Sociology of Personal Transformation." In *The Oxford Handbook of Cognitive Sociology*, edited by W. H. Brekhus and G. Ignatow, 623–42. New York: Oxford University Press.

DeGloma and Johnston examine the role of cognitive migrations in narrative identity work. Analyzing how people's sense of self migrates or shifts across the trajectory of the life course, they illustrate that identity is mobile and subject to significant movements and shifts across time.

Waters, Mary C. 1990. *Ethnic Options: Choosing Identities in America*. Berkeley: University of California Press.

Waters examines the mobility of white European ethnic identities. Showing first that at the societal level these identities have become less full-time and less salient, she also demonstrates that late-generation white European ethnics treat ethnicity as a symbolic, fluid, and optional resource that they can deploy in some spaces and submerge in others.

Doane, Ashley W. 1997. "Dominant Group Ethnic Identity in the United States: The Role of 'Hidden' Ethnicity in Intergroup Relations." *Sociological Quarterly* 38(3): 375–97.

Doane examines the evolution of dominant ethnic identity in the United States, showing that the boundaries of dominant group ethnicity shift in response to historical and social conditions. Often these boundaries broaden during periods of economic expansion and contract during periods of economic uncertainty.

Conclusion

How do authenticity, multidimensionality, and mobility relate to one another? We've seen that authenticity is a complex negotiation—and a fluid one, which can at times be about one's self and other times about some other, equally specific identity category. This fluidity can occur even within the same negotiation; for example, one may demonstrate punk or hip-hop authenticity by attempting to show that one is "naturally authentic" and is above socially produced, chameleonic conformities to a cultural code. Tensions between being and doing expressed in authenticity claims and disputes reflect on identity mobility, because the ability to show that one has some permanence in one's identity bolsters that person's authenticity claim. That said, transitory travelers in and out of identities can deploy context-specific forms of cultural capital in the right settings so as to assert authenticity without the permanent temporal grounding that some members and enforcers of identity categories demand. There are several important take-aways that one can draw from an exploration of identity that pays attention to individual and collective forms of authenticity, multi-dimensionality, and mobility.

Navigating Authenticities in Relation to Multidimensionality and Mobility

First, both individuals and collectives navigate authenticity in relation to multidimensionality and mobility. Introducing multidimensionality and mobility complicates widely held and enduring assumptions about authenticity. Authenticity in its most easily recognized analytic form seems pretty straightforward. The most authentic ethnic neighborhood is the longstanding enclave with a high percentage of people with a shared ethnicity that is different from the dominant group's ethnicity. The most authentic punk is the full-time high-density "real punk" who lives his or her identity, not the part-time "pretender." The most authentic gang-associated youth, and the one most likely to capture journalistic and ethnographic attention, is the full-time gang member who is always conspicuously involved in illegal activity. The most authentically gay person is an insider to a specifically gay subculture who lives and works in a gay enclave. These conceptions of who is the most authentic exemplar of something are widely held in popular culture and sometimes reproduced in scholarly communities as well. They are based on the assumption that full-time or long-term commitment (identity duration) and high-intensity differentiation from other categories (identity density) are the two central or core measures of authenticity. While these are often reflected as central by members with the most categorial capital to make their authenticity claims stick, authenticity is more complicated than this. There are multiple vocabularies of motive for authenticity. Recognizing that the most visible, conventional notions of authenticity, namely those centered on density and duration, correspond to only *one* type in a mosaic of authenticities avoids the common ethnographic pattern of seeking out the punks, the enclave ethnic immigrants, the enclave gays, and the urban African Americans as representative of marked communities in their most "pure," undiluted, and authentic form.

Multiple authenticities suggest that, while some may have greater dominance than others, authenticity is a negotiation. Cate Irvin (2017) draws attention to the intersections of multidimensionality, authenticity, and mobility in discussing how the gourmet food truck industry in New Orleans combined two forms of "original authenticity" (food truck and brick and mortar establishment) to create a temporal product, of *hybrid authenticity*. Using "original authenticity" to refer to dominant notions, where authenticity is based on length of duration and commitment to the relevant set of subcultural standards, Irvin shows that the blending of elements that were not part of the original standards created new, intersecting authenticities and hybrid places. Thus, for example, foreign foodie trucks were paired with dive bars in middle-class neighborhoods and down-home trucks were paired with upscale bars in minority neighborhoods, to craft unique forms of authenticity that attracted a different clientele from the one the businesses originally catered to. The merging of down-home trucks with upscale bars in a minority neighborhood lent a gritty, local authenticity to the upscale bar, which was seemingly out of place in the neighborhood; and the upscale bar lent polished "foodie" authenticity credentials to the food truck. This gave both a co-produced hybrid authenticity, temporally and spatially located.

The multidimensionality and mobility of authenticities also reminds one that not all authenticities are consciously and intentionally displayed. While analysts are often drawn to the most intentional constructions of ethnic or national pride and to the identity politics of social movement leaders, more banal displays of ethnicity, nationalism, and category membership may be enacted as authentic from the actor's point of view. Michael Billig's (1995) analysis of *banal nationalism*, according to which nationalism is quietly reproduced in everyday mundane acts and discourses—for example in the togetherness implicit in press outlets, in national songs at sporting events, and in terms such as *the* president, *the* weather, and *our* team—reminds one that acts that authenticate the nation need not be as overt as fervent movements of extremist nationalism. Billig even suggests that these more mundane forms of national identity construction are more powerful in authenticating a "national community" because, by comparison to marked forms of nationalism, their taken-for-grantedness hides their force to motivate political power and political violence.

Among individuals who navigate multiple authenticities through the fluid deployment of different identities in different contexts, it is not necessarily those with the most consciously and intentionally displayed identities who are experienced as the most authentic. Rios (2017) suggests, for example, that, in the gang-associated

Latino men he studied, the more variegated selves they performed across other contexts, when they were not putting up their tough gang personae in the face of distrusting authorities, were more representative of who they really are. For this reason, ethnographers who seek out the "most authentic" urban gang members are likely missing the multidimensionality of an authentic identity performance.

Multidimensionality and Fluidity Complicate Group and Place Identities

Multidimensionality and fluidity complicate categorial group and place identities. Chapter 2 discussed the idea of collective agency, according to which groups can act together in such a way as to show agreement, partly or mostly, upon shared definitions of who they are. Brubaker (2002) reminds us to consider "groupness" as a fluid process rather than "groups" as fixed entities. Thinking about collective categories in terms of their flexible saliences and levels of commitment from potential members helps us to keep in mind the complex and uneven negotiations of socially constructed categories. Considering how place identities intersect with group identities to make us who we are illuminates the interplay between multidimensionality and the places we inhabit. Recall how LGBQ identities in four small United States cities shaped how residents saw both their personal and their categorial identities in interaction with the places where they lived.

In another example of research that examines the intersections of place and identity, Iddo Tavory (2016) ethnographically explores the complicated issues of identification, groupness, and ethnic place in a tight-knit Orthodox Jewish community and neighborhood in Los Angeles. At one level, he analyzes what it means to be an Orthodox Jew in terms of social expectations from these people, and how being an Orthodox Jew organizes one's day and regulates one's identity in an ethnic enclave—a close community where one lives with other Orthodox Jews. But, veering away from an exclusive examination of the participants' identities through this lens of a classic ethnic enclave produced by a closed group, Tavory analyzes how Orthodox Jewish people navigate their identity in contact with non-Jewish members of the neighborhood.

Thus, unlike many ethnographic approaches that focus largely on the higher homogeneity of ethnic enclaves, he examines the interplay between the Orthodox ethnic community and the heterogeneous elements it intersects with. While the neighborhood is filled with synagogues, kosher restaurants, and an Orthodox Jewish presence, it is also populated with dive bars, hipster boutiques, expensive restaurants, and tattoo parlors; and, despite its large Jewish population, even more of its residents are non-Jewish. These non-Jewish residents and passers-through occupy the neighborhood and contribute to its overall vibe in a different way; they follow different social patterns. Rather than focus on the dense identity of Orthodox Jewish residents as a fixed characteristic, Tavory analyzes their embodied interactions, showing that, in following their routine habits and wearing visible markers such as yarmulkes, they are regularly "summoned" to their identity by a wide range of stimuli: encounters with other Jewish members, who follow the same habits, friendly small talk with non-Jewish others, the nod of strangers, and the rarer anti-Semitic remarks. As a result of their embodied daily habits, Orthodox Jewish residents, rather than putting on a conscious and intentional identity performance for non-Jewish residents, come to anticipate categorization and boundary-forming interactions of various kinds. Their identifications are interactionally fluid as identifications are assumed, forgotten, backgrounded, and rematerialized in the acts of others.

Identity and Marginality: Authenticity, Multidimensionality, and Mobility in Marginality Management

Identity is an important resource in navigating marginality and stigma. Actors with marginalizing attributes use authenticity, multidimensionality, and mobility to navigate these attributes. Denied access to full belonging in dominant or mainstream cultural settings, marginalized members develop alternative cultural capital and identity currencies that give them status, cultural prestige, and dignity in specific cultural contexts. Establishing authentication standards for full-fledged membership in oppositional subcultures, social movements of identity politics, or ethnic and racial communities creates symbolic group boundaries; group inclusion affords the potential for opposition or mobilization, confers status, and provides community membership.

People with marginalized identities navigate multidimensionality through mobile strategies of marginality management, bringing together different attributes of their identity in different configurations at different times and places. They code-switch identity currencies, presenting authentication standards for multiple memberships; they present the auxiliary characteristics for authentication in mainstream unmarked contexts, while switching to alternative cultural capitals for other settings.

Identity and Privilege: Authenticity, Multidimensionality, and Mobility in Privilege Management

I have emphasized identity and privilege management in addition to identity and marginality management. The literature on identity as a resource in privilege management is less extensive and more recent than the literature on marginality or stigma management, and this is so for a variety of reasons. Ethnographers are more likely to study how the socially marginalized navigate their worlds than how the socially advantaged negotiate their worlds. Many ethnographers trace their methodological roots to the Chicago School tradition of using the city as an urban laboratory in the study of deviant process and subcultural association within urban subcultures. It is also easier to gain access to people with less power than to people with more power. Additionally, sociological researchers often champion the underdog and seek out social movements or communities that navigate oppression. Standpoint theorists have emphasized the vantage points of the marginalized and how they manage their intersecting dimensions of marginality. Applying the valuable analytic tools of standpoint intersectionality to intersecting dimensions of privilege assists in demonstrating how the marginality of the marginalized is reproduced in the identity practices of people with privilege.

Authenticity is a resource that privileged members of a social category can use to define the rules of full access. Authenticity can restrict others' full inclusion and access to resources. What it means to be authentically American, for example, is an authenticity question with significant implications. Navigating multidimensionality is an important element in privilege management. Most actors have a mixture of privileging and marginalizing statuses; and the ability to deploy their privileging attributes to gain social advantage allows actors to negotiate their own identities in ways that are personally advantageous, even as they reproduce the power of privilege. The mobility of identities means that actors who are significantly disadvantaged in one context can still reproduce structures of privilege in another context.

Privilege is reproduced through both conscious and unconscious identity practice. Identity practices run along a continuum from strongly intentional presentations of identity (deliberate, conscious impression management strategies) to largely unconscious and tacit identity practices (embodied, automatic, unconscious activities that enact one's identity). At the conscious end of the spectrum, direct and visible acts of intentional symbolic differentiation between the privileged and the marginalized are conscious identity management strategies that reproduce privilege. When privileged people bully members of an out-group in order to mark through violence that group's subordinate status, when they define outsiders as moral pollutants, and when they erect exclusivist authenticity standards, all these behaviors are largely conscious identity strategies. But the privileged also reproduce their advantages in embodied, taken-for-granted practices of doing identity that they are not fully aware of. A middle-class white woman who hires one out of several qualified applicants on the basis of a letter of recommendation from a white colleague within her mostly white middle-class social network, or who chooses a neighborhood for her son that will allow that child to attend a good school, is performing an intersectional white middle-class identity and reproducing race and class as everyday identity practice; but her strategic use of identity as a resource is relatively unconscious rather than a conspicuously deliberate performance of identity.

Identity Play and Provisional Identities: Connecting Mobility with Multidimensionality and Authenticity

The tacit practice of doing unconscious, taken-for-granted, and unmarked identities represents what we might call identity routine.

The more conscious practices of doing identity might be called identity work and identity play. Much of the research on identity authenticity and multidimensionality has focused on the identity work that people with solid commitments to an identity engage in. Thus authenticity accounts usually focus on the standards of authentication devised by longstanding cultural insiders whose commitment to an enduring duration, or even to the appearance of an essentialist permanence, is a significant authentication requirement. Provisional identities require analytic attention as potential bridges to enduring identities. Understandably, cultural insiders committed to duration dismiss temporary identities as less serious and possibly inauthentic, but this does not mean that analysts should ignore these identities or accept the cultural insider's view as their own position.

The enactment of provisional, transitory, part-time identities has a number of uses. Navigating the different cultural capitals of multiple identities can produce a kind of multicultural capital that allows one to move between social worlds and accumulate different rewards, ranging from context-specific prestige in one setting to the privilege of unmarked normality in another and to the ability to try on and experience a new attribute of self in yet another setting. Provisional selves are temporally mobile and transitory, but these part-time enactments allow actors to consider broader migrations to new permanent identities.

Identity play occurs at the collective level as well. Cities and neighborhoods, through their community identity entrepreneurs, may experiment with provisional new identities, trying to appeal, for example, to a more hip, artistic vibe in a gritty, post-industrial area. The experiment may fail to change the city's or neighborhood's central identity, or it may contribute to a long-term migration to a fundamentally different city or neighborhood identity. Organizations may similarly experiment with provisional changes to their identity or brand. The hybrid authenticities that developed in New Orleans's gourmet food truck and restaurant industries—from the identity play of navigating multidimensionality through moving food trucks into neighborhoods at night, when they were paired with other styles of "authentic" places—have led to an organizational migration and resettlement into a new, more hybrid identity.

Key Areas for Future Research in Identity Authenticity, Multidimensionality, and Mobility

Where does identity research go from here? How should researchers continue to analyze the relationships between authenticities, multidimensionality, and mobility? If you are a scholar newly interested in the study of identity, what are some interesting possibilities to consider? On the basis of the more promising avenues of current scholarship, the possible future of world events, and corresponding trends in sociology, I offer some brief suggestions.

Disruption and its effects on identity is a topic of growing importance, both for its dramatic realities and for its analytic possibilities (see also Fine and Tavory 2019: 463–4 on disruption in symbolic interaction). Disruptions that range from increasing group conflicts to economic shifts, to changing migration patterns, to global pandemics, or to climate change threaten our stability and have significant implications for identity. Early symbolic interactionists emphasized harmonious group relations (Fine and Tavory 2019: 463), and early Meadean views of the self similarly assumed harmony. Harmony and stability are still important features of social life; but it is hard to look at the current world, or at the future, and not see the potential for disharmony and disruption. Although often challenging to live through, disruptions provide a fruitful avenue for studying identity. How is authenticity constructed during conflicts and changes in the social order? How do the rules for authenticity change, and how do people adapt to those changes? How, for instance, does migration affect identity authentication when someone moves from one place to the next? How does migration affect the identity of the places that gain migrants and the identity of the places that lose migrants? We have seen that disruptions caused by changing neighborhood composition have led to negotiated shifts in authenticity and to the creation of "hybrid authenticities" in New Orleans's businesses. What other kinds of hybrid authenticities are brought about through new migration patterns? How does migration prompt communities to reimagine their own identities?

How will the disruptions caused by climate change affect the identity of people and places? How will places reinvent themselves after disasters, droughts, migrations, or other effects of climate change? One promising example of identity research tying climate change to identity multidimensionality and mobility is Leap's (2019) analysis of how Sumner, Missouri, the "wild goose capital of the world," has had to readapt its community identity, and how men in the community have had to reimagine their masculine identities, in the face of the loss of 99% of their migrant goose numbers because of changes in goose migration patterns caused by climate and land use changes. Leap demonstrates that rural masculinities are complex and intersectional: men who lost goose hunting as a status marker adapted in ways that allowed them to continue doing masculinities associated with an acceptable "unmarked" race (white) and class (middle). They replaced goose hunting with new forms of hunt, associated with middle-class respectability, and avoided other forms, associated with the lower classes. As an example of research on identity adaptation, Leap's study reminds us that social change produced by disruption is ripe for identity study. Identity adaptations associated with disruption afford researchers a chance to observe the development of new markers of authenticity, shifts and mobility in presentations of identity, and the navigation of intersectionality in new ways.

As countries mobilize in the face of the coronavirus pandemic, how does a global virus affect the identity of the nations that it disrupts? Does the "imagined community" come together in important, identity-affirming ways, or is it fractured as its many members clash over the ways in which the virus reveals the "winners" and "losers" in the social order? How do nations and their people respond to one another? Do they form symbolic boundaries and try to avoid contact with nations and individuals marked with the stigma of being likely vectors? Pandemics offer the potential to analyze the effects of disruption on the identities of collectives and the symbolic boundary strategies of individuals and collectives.

Even as disruption and large-scale social problems threaten to shape significant chunks of the future, it is still important to continue to study the mundane as well as the obviously consequential and exotic. The affinities between intersectionality, with its explicit concern with marginalities, and multidimensionality, with its interest in the negotiations of marginality and privilege and in their relationships to mobility, continue to be worthy of further exploration. As sociologists of the self and symbolic interactionists have become increasingly interested in inequalities, there is a need to explore the entire range of continua of social locations, from the multiply disadvantaged to the multiply privileged. We have seen in some of the ethnographic examples discussed that, despite constraints, people develop strategies to balance their marked and unmarked identity attributes. Researchers should stay attuned to how people may deploy identity as a resource, both in stigma-managing ways and in privilege-reinforcing ways. Understanding that there are multiple authenticities and vocabularies of motive for doing identity, it is important to attend to the element of in-group variation when we judge how authenticating moves are made and what vocabularies of motive count and do not count.

Given that the online world and the physical world shape each other, there are expanding opportunities to study the fluidity of identity and authenticity in online spaces. One avenue to explore, for example, is how "expert authenticity" is established in the absence of formal credentialing, in cases where online groups answer the questions of social media users who seek out "expert answers" in the context of an online group with "experts." Whom do Facebook users trust to be an "authentic expert" when they ask for a travel recommendation, or gardening advice, or advice on whom to select for their fantasy football team? To what degree does having or appearing to have racial, gender, and social class characteristics similar to those of the questioner influence the questioner's trust? What characteristics are valued in online experts, and are they more related to one's marked and unmarked appearance attributes or to one's performance of belonging to a particular online community? On Facebook, for example, there are multiple groups where you can ask someone to identify a snake in your yard, or you can discuss the recruits and coaching of a sports team, or you can get gardening advice. Administrators of such groups have an icon of a badge next to their name, and this badge distinguishes them from ordinary members of the group. The badges operate as signifiers of "expertise," even if the credentials needed for acquiring a badge are as simple as starting the group, or being invited to be an administrator by another group administrator. In this context, how do these "online experts" become respected authorities in a community? Who respects and who questions their authority? Is the badge enough? And what causes people to be "de-badged"? What disputes over expertise and group identity shape such communities? How do people establish authenticity across competing groups and within their own group? How do these groups themselves become identity communities centered around seeking and providing information, as a source of group belonging?

In thinking about avenues for further research, it may be useful to consider how authenticity, multidimensionality, and mobility shape your own social networks and presentations of identity. Contemplating the role of identity in your own social worlds opens up possibilities for considering the many different ways in which the concepts of authenticity, multidimensionality, and mobility relate to one another.

Analyzing Authenticity, Multidimensionality, and Mobility in Your Own Lives

Identities are negotiated by performing authenticity or standards of authentication. We often deploy identity in a flexible and fluid manner, presenting, accentuating, and deemphasizing various attributes of privilege and marginality in different configurations across different times and spaces and around different people. We can fluidly balance the multidimensional attributes of our self by mobilizing its different aspects as we change environments. We can also combine several attributes in complex ways, which allow us to present our multidimensionality together, in one coherent, if hybrid, whole. We can enact an intersectional class-related, ethnicized, racial, gendered, regional, age-related, national, subcultural, and occupational identity all at once, as a single performance that combines elements of unintentional identity routine with conscious identity work and play.

As you consider your own identities, the identities of others around you, the identities of the places and organizations you encounter, your categories of belonging, and your nation, you can attend to the issues of authenticity, multidimensionality, and mobility. How do you define your personal authenticity? What standards of authentication do you follow when establishing your membership in the groups or subcultures you belong to? How do you navigate the multiple attributes of marginalization and privilege that you possess? How do you try to balance them? In what instances do you deploy your privilege, either consciously, to

gain strategic rewards, or unconsciously, without much consideration, as a part of daily habit? How do you use time and space to
negotiate your identity attributes? Do you present yourself differently in different social circles and in different times and spaces?
What identities are you trying on in a transitory, fluid manner?
What identities do you experience as permanent and enduring?
Exploring these questions in the context of how identity plays out
in your lives and around you will help to illuminate the complexities of identity as an intensely social process.

References

Alba, Richard D. 1990. *Ethnic Identity: The Transformation of White America*. New Haven, CT: Yale University Press.

Anderson, Benedict. 1983. *Imagined Communities: Reflections on the Origin and Spread of Nationalism*. London: Verso.

Anspach, Renee R. 1979. "From Stigma to Identity Politics: Political Activism among the Physically Disabled and Former Mental Patients." *Social Science & Medicine, Part A: Medical Psychology & Medical Sociology* 13: 765–73.

Armstrong, Elizabeth A., and Laura T. Hamilton. 2015. *Paying for the Party: How College Maintains Inequality*. Cambridge, MA: Harvard University Press.

Barth, Fredrik (ed.). 1969. *Ethnic Groups and Boundaries: The Social Organization of Culture Difference*. Boston, MA: Little, Brown & Co.

Benford, Robert D., and David A. Snow. 2000. "Framing Processes and Social Movements: An Overview and Assessment." *Annual Review of Sociology* 26(1): 611–39.

Bernstein, Mary. 2005. "Identity Politics." *Annual Review of Sociology* 31(1): 47–74.

Bettie, Julie. 2000. "Women without Class: Chicas, Cholas, Trash, and the Presence/Absence of Class Identity." *Signs* 26(1): 1–35.

Bettie, Julie. 2014. *Women without Class: Girls, Race, and Identity*. Oakland: University of California Press.

Beverland, Michael B. 2005. "Crafting Brand Authenticity: The

Case of Luxury Wines." *Journal of Management Studies* 42(5): 1003–29.

Billig, Michael. 1995. *Banal Nationalism*. London: SAGE.

Binder, Amy. 1999. "Friend and Foe: Boundary Work and Collective Identity in the Afrocentric and Multicultural Curriculum Movements in American Public Education," pp. 221–48 in *The Cultural Territories of Race: Black and White Boundaries*, edited by M. Lamont. Chicago, IL: University of Chicago Press.

Blumer, Herbert. 1969. *Symbolic Interactionism: Perspective and Method*. Englewood Cliffs, NJ: Prentice Hall.

Bottero, Wendy. 2010. "Intersubjectivity and Bourdieusian Approaches to 'Identity.'" *Cultural Sociology* 4(1): 3–22.

Bourdieu, Pierre. 1984. *Distinction: A Social Critique of the Judgement of Taste*. Cambridge, MA: Harvard University Press.

Bourdieu, Pierre, and Loïc J. D. Wacquant. 2002 [1992]. *An Invitation to Reflexive Sociology*. Cambridge: Polity.

Brekhus, Wayne H. 1996. "Social Marking and the Mental Coloring of Identity: Sexual Identity Construction and Maintenance in the United States." *Sociological Forum* 11(3): 497–522.

Brekhus, Wayne H. 1998. "A Sociology of the Unmarked: Redirecting Our Focus." *Sociological Theory* 16(1): 34–51.

Brekhus, Wayne H. 2003. *Peacocks, Chameleons, Centaurs: Gay Suburbia and the Grammar of Social Identity*. Chicago, IL: University of Chicago Press.

Brekhus, Wayne H. 2007. "The Rutgers School: A Zerubavelian Culturalist Cognitive Sociology." *European Journal of Social Theory* 10(3): 448–64.

Brekhus, Wayne H. 2008. "Trends in the Qualitative Study of Social Identities." *Sociology Compass* 2(3): 1059–78.

Brekhus, Wayne H. 2015. *Culture and Cognition: Patterns in the Social Construction of Reality*. Cambridge: Polity.

Brekhus, Wayne H., and Gabe Ignatow. 2019. "Cognitive Sociology and the Cultural Mind: Debates, Directions, and Challenges," pp. 1–27 in *The Oxford Handbook of Cognitive Sociology*, edited by W. H. Brekhus and G. Ignatow. New York: Oxford University Press.

Brown-Saracino, Japonica. 2018. *How Places Make Us: Novel LBQ Identities in Four Small Cities*. Chicago, IL: University of Chicago Press.

Brubaker, Rogers. 1992. *Citizenship and Nationhood in France and Germany*. Cambridge, MA: Harvard University Press.

Brubaker, Rogers. 2002. "Ethnicity without Groups." *European Journal of Sociology / Archives Européennes de Sociologie* 43(2): 163–89.

Brubaker, Rogers. 2006. *Ethnicity without Groups*. Cambridge, MA: Harvard University Press.

Brubaker, Rogers, and Frederick Cooper. 2000. "Beyond 'Identity.'" *Theory and Society* 29(1): 1–47.

Brubaker, Rogers, Mara Loveman, and Peter Stamatov. 2004. "Ethnicity as Cognition." *Theory and Society* 33(1): 31–64.

Bryson, Bethany. 1996. "'Anything but Heavy Metal': Symbolic Exclusion and Musical Dislikes." *American Sociological Review* 61(5): 884–99.

Burke, Peter J., and Jan E. Stets. 2009. *Identity Theory*. New York: Oxford University Press.

Butler, Judith. 1990. *Gender Trouble: Feminism and the Subversion of Identity*. New York: Routledge.

Cairns, James Irvine. 2017. *The Myth of the Age of Entitlement: Millennials, Austerity, and Hope*. North York, Ontario: University of Toronto Press.

Campion, Lisa. 2019. "Doing Identity: A Social Pattern Analysis Exploring the Process of Identity Construction and Maintenance." PhD dissertation, Rutgers University, New Brunswick, New Jersey.

Carroll, Glenn R., and Dennis Ray Wheaton. 2009. "The Organizational Construction of Authenticity: An Examination of Contemporary Food and Dining in the US." *Research in Organizational Behavior* 29: 255–82.

Carter, Michael J., and Celene Fuller. 2015. "Symbolic Interactionism." *Sociopedia.isa*. doi: 10.1177/205684601561.

Carter, Prudence L. 2003. "'Black'" Cultural Capital, Status Positioning, and Schooling Conflicts for Low-Income African American Youth." *Social Problems* 50(1): 136–55.

Cerulo, Karen A. 1997. "Identity Construction: New Issues, New Directions." *Annual Review of Sociology* 23(1): 385–409.

Chayko, Mary. 2017. *Superconnected: The Internet, Digital Media, and Techno-Social Life*. Los Angeles, CA: SAGE.

Chodrow, Nancy. 1978. *The Reproduction of Mothering:*

Psychoanalysis and the Sociology of Gender. Berkeley: University of California Press.

Cooley, Charles Horton. 1964 [1902]. *Human Nature and the Social Order.* New York: Schocken Books.

Crenshaw, Kimberlé. 1991. "Mapping the Margins: Intersectionality, Identity Politics, and Violence against Women of Color." *Stanford Law Review* 43(6): 1241–99.

Davis, Joseph E. 2011. "The Shifting Experience of Self." *Hedgehog Review* (Spring). https://hedgehogreview.com/issues/the-shifting-experience-of-self/articles/the-shifting-experience-of-self-a-bibliographic-essay.

De Fina, Anna. 2003. *Identity in Narrative: A Study of Immigrant Discourse.* Amsterdam: John Benjamins.

DeGloma, Thomas. 2014. *Seeing the Light: The Social Logic of Personal Discovery.* Chicago, IL: University of Chicago Press.

DeGloma, Thomas, and Erin F. Johnston. 2019. "Cognitive Migrations: A Cultural and Cognitive Sociology of Personal Transformation," pp. 623–42 in *The Oxford Handbook of Cognitive Sociology,* edited by W. H. Brekhus and G. Ignatow. New York: Oxford University Press.

Desmond, Matthew. 2007. *On the Fireline: Living and Dying with Wildland Firefighters.* Chicago, IL: University of Chicago Press.

DiMaggio, Paul. 1997. "Culture and Cognition." *Annual Review of Sociology* 23(1): 263–87.

Doane, Ashley W. 1997. "Dominant Group Ethnic Identity in the United States: The Role of 'Hidden' Ethnicity in Intergroup Relations." *Sociological Quarterly* 38(3): 375–97.

Dudley, David. 2019. "How Helsinki Built 'Book Heaven.'" CityLab. https://www.citylab.com/design/2019/11/finland-public-library-photos-helsinki-books-nordic-culture/601192.

Dyer, Richard. 1988. "White." *Screen* 29(4): 44–65.

Erickson, Bonnie. 2003. "Social Networks: The Value of Variety." *Contexts* 2(1): 25–31.

Erikson, Erik Homburger. 1994 [1959]. *Identity and the Life Cycle.* New York: W. W. Norton.

Fenton, Steve. 2011. "The Sociology of Ethnicity and National Identity." *Ethnicities* 11(1): 12–17.

Fine, Gary Alan. 1979. "Small Groups and Culture Creation: The Idioculture of Little League Baseball Teams." *American Sociological Review* 44(5): 733–45.

Fine, Gary Alan. 2003. "Towards a Peopled Ethnography: Developing Theory from Group Life." *Ethnography* 4(1): 41–60.

Fine, Gary Alan. 2012. "Group Culture and the Interaction Order: Local Sociology on the Meso-Level." *Annual Review of Sociology* 38(1): 159–79.

Fine, Gary Alan, and Iddo Tavory. 2019. "Interactionism in the Twenty-First Century: A Letter on Being-in-a-Meaningful-World." *Symbolic Interaction* 42(3): 457–67.

Force, William Ryan. 2009. "Consumption Styles and the Fluid Complexity of Punk Authenticity." *Symbolic Interaction* 32(4): 289–309.

Fox, Kathryn Joan. 1987. "Real Punks and Pretenders: The Social Organization of a Counterculture." *Journal of Contemporary Ethnography* 16(3): 344–70.

Frankenberg, Ruth. 1993. *White Women, Race Matters: The Social Construction of Whiteness*. Minneapolis: University of Minnesota Press.

Gamson, William. 1992. "The Social Psychology of Collective Action," pp. 53–76 in *Frontiers in Social Movement Theory*, edited by A. Morris and C. Mueller. New Haven, CT: Yale University Press.

Gamson, William A., Bruce Fireman, and Steven Rytina. 1982. *Encounters with Unjust Authority*. Homewood, IL: Dorsey Press.

Garfinkel, Harold. 1967. *Studies in Ethnomethodology*. Englewood Cliffs, NJ: Prentice Hall.

Garroutte, Eva Marie. 2003. *Real Indians: Identity and the Survival of Native America*. Berkeley: University of California Press.

Gaytan, Marie Sarita. 2008. "From Sombreros to Sincronizadas: Authenticity, Ethnicity, and the Mexican Restaurant Industry." *Journal of Contemporary Ethnography* 37(3): 314–41.

Gergen, Kenneth J. 1991. *The Saturated Self: Dilemmas of Identity in Contemporary Life*. New York: Basic Books.

Ghaziani, Amin. 2015. *There Goes the Gayborhood?* Princeton, NJ: Princeton University Press.

Gitlin, Todd. 1996. *The Twilight of Common Dreams: Why America Is Wracked by Culture Wars*. New York: Holt.

Goffman, Erving. 1959. *The Presentation of Self in Everyday Life*. New York: Anchor.

Goffman, Erving. 1961. *Asylums: Essays on the Social Situation of Mental Patients and Other Inmates.* New York: Anchor Books.

Goffman, Erving. 1974. *Frame Analysis: An Essay on the Organization of Experience.* New York: Harper & Row.

Goffman, Erving. 1986 [1963]. *Stigma: Notes on the Management of Spoiled Identity.* New York: Touchstone.

Grazian, David. 2003. *Blue Chicago: The Search for Authenticity in Urban Blues Clubs.* Chicago, IL: University of Chicago Press.

Grazian, David. 2008. *On the Make: The Hustle of Urban Nightlife.* Chicago, IL: University of Chicago Press.

Gubrium, Jaber F. 2005. "Introduction: Narrative Environments and Social Problems." *Social Problems* 52(4): 525–8.

Gubrium, Jaber F., and James A. Holstein. 2000. "The Self in a World of Going Concerns." *Symbolic Interaction* 23(2): 95–115.

Hagerman, Margaret A. 2018. *White Kids: Growing Up with Privilege in a Racially Divided America.* New York: New York University Press.

Harter, Susan. 1997. "The Personal Self in Social Context: Barriers to Authenticity," pp. 81–105 in *Self and Identity: Fundamental Issues*, edited by R. D. Ashmore and L. Jussim. Oxford: Oxford University Press.

Hartsock, Nancy C. M. 1983. *Money, Sex, and Power: Toward a Feminist Historical Materialism.* New York: Longman.

Hennen, Peter. 2008. *Faeries, Bears, and Leathermen: Men in Community Queering the Masculine.* Chicago, IL: University of Chicago Press.

Herb, Guntram H. 1999. "National Identity and Territory," pp. 9–30 in *Nested Identities: Nationalism, Territory, and Scale*, edited by G. H. Herb and D. H. Kaplan. Lanham, MD: Rowman & Littlefield.

Hill Collins, Patricia. 2009. *Black Feminist Thought: Knowledge, Consciousness, and the Politics of Empowerment* (2nd edn.). New York: Routledge.

Hill Collins, Patricia. 2019. *Intersectionality as Critical Social Theory.* Durham, NC: Duke University Press.

Hill Collins, Patricia, and Sirma Bilge. 2016. *Intersectionality.* Cambridge: Polity.

Hoover, Eric. 2009. "The Millennial Muddle: How Stereotyping Students Became a Thriving Industry and a Bundle of Contradictions." *Chronicle of Higher Education*, October 11.

https://www.chronicle.com/article/The-Millennial-Muddle-How/48772.

Howard, Judith A. 2000. "Social Psychology of Identities." *Annual Review of Sociology* 26(1): 367–93.

Hughes, Everett C. 1945. "Dilemmas and Contradictions of Status." *American Journal of Sociology* 50(5): 353–9.

Ibarra, Herminia, and Jennifer L. Petriglieri. 2010. "Identity Work and Play." *Journal of Organizational Change Management* 23(1): 10–25.

Irvin, Cate. 2017. "Constructing Hybridized Authenticities in the Gourmet Food Truck Scene: Constructing Hybridized Authenticities." *Symbolic Interaction* 40(1): 43–62.

Jacobs, Michelle R., and David M. Merolla. 2017. "Being Authentically American Indian: Symbolic Identity Construction and Social Structure among Urban New Indians." *Symbolic Interaction* 40(1): 63–82.

Jasper, James M. 1997. *The Art of Moral Protest: Culture, Biography, and Creativity in Social Movements*. Chicago, IL: University of Chicago Press.

Jenkins, Richard. 1996. *Social Identity*. London: Routledge.

Jenkins, Richard. 2014. *Social Identity* (4th edn.). New York: Routledge.

Johnston, Erin F. 2013. "'I Was Always This Way…': Rhetorics of Continuity in Narratives of Conversion." *Sociological Forum* 28(3): 549–73.

Johnston, Josée, and Shyon Baumann. 2007. "Democracy versus Distinction: A Study of Omnivorousness in Gourmet Food Writing." *American Journal of Sociology* 113(1): 165–204.

Kalish, Rachel, and Michael Kimmel. 2010. "Suicide by Mass Murder: Masculinity, Aggrieved Entitlement, and Rampage School Shootings." *Health Sociology Review* 19(4): 451–64.

Kauffman, L. A. 1990. "The Anti-Politics of Identity." *Socialist Review* 20(1): 67–80.

Kefalas, Maria. 2003. *Working-Class Heroes: Protecting Home, Community, and Nation in a Chicago Neighborhood*. Berkeley: University of California Press.

Kiely, Richard, Frank Bechhofer, Robert Stewart, and David McCrone. 2001. "The Markers and Rules of Scottish National Identity." *Sociological Review* 49(1): 33–55.

Kimmel, Michael. 2002. "Gender, Class, and Terrorism."

Chronicle of Higher Education, February 8. https://www. chronicle.com/article/Gender-ClassTerrorism/6096.

King, Deborah K. 1988. "Multiple Jeopardy, Multiple Consciousness: The Context of a Black Feminist Ideology." *Signs: Journal of Women in Culture and Society* 14(1): 42–72.

Kirkpatrick, David. 2011. *The Facebook Effect: The Inside Story of the Company That Is Connecting the World*. New York: Simon & Schuster.

Lamia, Mary C. 2010. "Do Bullies Really Have Low Self-Esteem?" *Psychology Today*, October 22. https://www.psychologytoday. com/us/blog/intense-emotions-and-strong-feelings/201010/do-bullies-really-have-low-self-esteem.

Lamont, Michèle. l992. *Money, Morals, and Manners: The Culture of the French and American Upper-Middle Class*. Chicago, IL: University of Chicago Press.

Lamont, Michèle. 2000. *The Dignity of Working Men: Morality and the Boundaries of Race, Class, and Immigration*. New York: Russell Sage Foundation.

Lamont, Michèle, and Virág Molnár. 2002. "The Study of Boundaries Across the Social Sciences." *Annual Review of Sociology* 28: 167–95.

Lawler, Steph. 2008. *Identity: Sociological Perspectives*. Cambridge: Polity.

Leap, Braden. 2017. "Survival Narratives: Constructing an Intersectional Masculinity through Stories of the Rural/Urban Divide." *Journal of Rural Studies* 55: 12–21.

Leap, Braden T. 2019. *Gone Goose: The Remaking of an American Town in the Age of Climate Change*. Philadelphia, PA: Temple University Press.

Levine, Martin P. 1979. "Gay Ghetto." *Journal of Homosexuality* 4(4): 363–77.

Li, Qian, and Xiaoli Tian. Forthcoming. "The Presence, Performance, and Politics of Online Interaction," in *The Oxford Handbook of Symbolic Interaction*, edited by W. H. Brekhus, T. DeGloma, and W. R. Force. New York: Oxford University Press.

Lindberg, Pirkko. 2016. "New Library Act and New Strategy for Finnish Public Libraries." IFLA Public Libraries Section Blog, June 1. http://blogs.ifla.org/public-libraries/2016/06/01/new-lib rary-act-and-new-strategy-for-finnish-public-libraries.

Lu, Shun, and Gary Alan Fine. 1995. "The Presentation of Ethnic Authenticity: Chinese Food as a Social Accomplishment." *Sociological Quarterly* 36(3): 535–53.

Mallea, Amahia. 2019. Book Review of *Wide-Open Town: Kansas City and the Pendergast Era*, edited by D. M. Burke, J. Roe, and J. Herron. *Missouri Historical Review* 114(1): 69–70.

McKinzie, Ashleigh E. 2017. "A Tale of Two Cities: Variations in Perceptions of Disaster Recovery and the Importance of Intersectionality." *Sociology of Race and Ethnicity* 3(4): 522–37.

McLean, Paul Douglas. 2017. *Culture in Networks*. Cambridge: Polity.

McLeod, Kembrew. 1999. "Authenticity within Hip-Hop and Other Cultures Threatened with Assimilation." *Journal of Communication* 49(4): 134–50.

Mead, George Herbert, and Charles W. Morris. 1967 [1934]. *Mind, Self and Society from the Standpoint of a Social Behaviorist*. Chicago, IL: University of Chicago Press.

Melbin, Murray. 1987. *Night as Frontier: Colonizing the World after Dark*. New York / London: Free Press / Collier Macmillan.

Mills, C. Wright. 1940. "Situated Actions and Vocabularies of Motive." *American Sociological Review* 5(6): 904–13.

Mullaney, Jamie L. 2006. *Everyone Is NOT Doing It: Abstinence and Personal Identity*. Chicago, IL: University of Chicago Press.

Nagel, Joane. 1994. "Constructing Ethnicity: Creating and Recreating Ethnic Identity and Culture." *Social Problems* 41(1): 152–76.

Nash, Jennifer C. 2008. "Re-Thinking Intersectionality." *Feminist Review* 89(1): 1–15.

Nippert-Eng, Christena E. 1996. *Home and Work: Negotiating Boundaries through Everyday Life*. Chicago, IL: University of Chicago Press.

Noah, Trevor. 2016. *Born a Crime: Stories from a South African Childhood*. New York: Spiegel & Grau.

Olzak, Susan. 1993. *The Dynamics of Ethnic Competition and Conflict*. Stanford, CA: Stanford University Press.

Owens, Timothy J., Dawn T. Robinson, and Lynn Smith-Lovin. 2010. "Three Faces of Identity." *Annual Review of Sociology* 36(1): 477–99.

Pachucki, Mark A., Sabrina Pendergrass, and Michèle Lamont.

2007. "Boundary Processes: Recent Theoretical Developments and New Contributions." *Poetics* 35(6): 331–51.

Pascoe, C. J. 2013. "Bullying as Social Inequality." *The Enemy.* http://theenemyreader.org/bullying-as-social-inequality.

Peeters, Margot, Antonius H. N. Cillessen, and Ron H. J. Scholte. 2010. "Clueless or Powerful? Identifying Subtypes of Bullies in Adolescence." *Journal of Youth and Adolescence* 39(9): 1041–52.

Perry, Pamela. 2001. "White Means Never Having to Say You're Ethnic." *Journal of Contemporary Ethnography* 30(1): 56–92.

Polletta, Francesca, and James M. Jasper. 2001. "Collective Identity and Social Movements." *Annual Review of Sociology* 27(1): 283–305.

Prins, Jacomijne, Jacquelien van Stekelenburg, Francesca Polletta, and Bert Klandermans. 2013. "Telling the Collective Story? Moroccan-Dutch Young Adults' Negotiation of a Collective Identity through Storytelling." *Qualitative Sociology* 36(1): 81–99.

Raphael, Michael W. 2017. "Cognitive Sociology." *Oxford Bibliographies Online in Sociology.* doi: 10.1093/obo/978019 9756384-0187.

Rhodes, Richard. 1987. "Cupcake Land: Requiem for the Midwest in the Key of Vanilla." *Harper's Magazine* 275(1650): 51–7.

Ribas, Vanesa. 2016. *On the Line: Slaughterhouse Lives and the Making of the New South.* Oakland: University of California Press.

Riesman, David. 1950. *The Lonely Crowd: A Study of the Changing American Character.* New Haven, CT: Yale University Press.

Rios, Victor M. 2017. *Human Targets: Schools, Police, and the Criminalization of Latino Youth.* Chicago, IL: University of Chicago Press.

Rockquemore, Kerry, and David L. Brunsma. 2002. *Beyond Black: Biracial Identity in America.* Thousand Oaks, CA: SAGE.

Schelling, Thomas C. 1971. "Dynamic Models of Segregation." *Journal of Mathematical Sociology* 1(2): 143–86.

Schwartz, Barry. 1997. "Collective Memory and History: How Abraham Lincoln Became a Symbol of Racial Equality." *Sociological Quarterly* 38(3): 469–96.

Scott, Rebecca R. 2010. *Removing Mountains: Extracting Nature and Identity in the Appalachian Coalfields.* Minneapolis: University of Minnesota Press.

Shelby, Tommie. 2002. "Foundations of Black Solidarity: Collective Identity or Common Oppression?" *Ethics* 112(2): 231–66.

Shenk, Petra Scott. 2007. "'I'm Mexican, Remember?' Constructing Ethnic Identities via Authenticating Discourse." *Journal of Sociolinguistics* 11(2): 194–220.

Shils, Edward. 1988. "Center and Periphery: An Idea and its Career, 1935–1987," pp. 250–82 in *Center: Ideas and Institutions*, edited by L. Greenfield and M. Martin. Chicago, IL: University of Chicago Press.

Sileo, Tom. 2016. "Attention, Millennials: The Real World Is Not a 'Safe Space.'" *The Stream*, November 15. https://stream.org/attention-millennials-the-world-is-not-a-safe-space.

Silver, Nate. 2008. "'Real' America Looks Different to Palin, Obama." *Five Thirty Eight*, October 18. https://fivethirtyeight.com/features/real-america-looks-different-to-palin.

Simmel, Georg. 1969 [1955]. *The Web of Group Affiliations*, translated by Kurt H. Wolff. Glencoe, IL: Free Press.

Smith, Dorothy E. 1987. *The Everyday World as Problematic: A Feminist Sociology.* Boston, MA: Northeastern University Press.

Snow, David A., and Robert D. Benford. 1988. "Ideology, Frame Resonance, and Participant Mobilization," pp. 197–217 in *From Structure to Action: Comparing Social Movement Research across Cultures*, edited by B. Klandermans, H. Kriesi, and S. G. Tarrow. Greenwich, CT: JAI Press.

Snow, David A., E. Burke Rochford, Jr., Steven K. Worden, and Robert D. Benford. 1986. "Frame Alignment Processes, Micromobilization, and Movement Participation." *American Sociological Review* 51(4): 464–81.

Snyder, Mark. 1987. *Public Appearances, Private Realities: The Psychology of Self-Monitoring.* New York: W. H. Freeman.

Spillman, Lyn. 1997. *Nation and Commemoration: Creating National Identities in the United States and Australia.* Cambridge: Cambridge University Press.

Spragens, Thomas A., Jr. 1999. "Identity Politics and the Liberalism of Difference." *Responsive Community* 9(3): 12–25.

Stein, Arlene. 1997. *Sex and Sensibility: Stories of a Lesbian Generation.* Berkeley: University of California Press.

Stein, Karen. 2019. *Getting Away from It All: Vacations and Identity*. Philadelphia, PA: Temple University Press.

Stets, Jan E., and Peter J. Burke. 1996. "Gender, Control, and Interaction." *Social Psychology Quarterly* 59(3): 193–220.

Stone, Gregory. 1962. "Apperance and the Self," pp. 86–118 in *Human Behavior and Social Processes: An Interactionist Approach*, edited by Arnold Marshall Rose. Boston, MA: Houghton Mifflin.

Stroud, Angela. 2012. "Good Guys with Guns: Hegemonic Masculinity and Concealed Handguns." *Gender & Society* 26(2): 216–38.

Stroud, Angela. 2015. *Good Guys with Guns: The Appeal and Consequences of Concealed Carry*. Chapel Hill: University of North Carolina Press.

Stryker, Sheldon. 1980. *Symbolic Interactionism: A Social Structural Version*. Menlo Park, CA: Benjamin/Cummings.

Stryker, Sheldon. 2008. "From Mead to a Structural Symbolic Interactionism and Beyond." *Annual Review of Sociology* 34(1): 15–31.

Stryker, Sheldon, and Peter J. Burke. 2000. "The Past, Present, and Future of an Identity Theory." *Social Psychology Quarterly* 63(4): 284–97.

Stryker, Sheldon, and Richard T. Serpe. 1982. "Commitment, Identity Salience, and Role Behavior: Theory and Research Example," pp. 199–218 in *Personality, Roles, and Social Behavior, Springer Series in Social Psychology*, edited by W. Ickes and E. S. Knowles. New York: Springer.

Sugrue, Thomas J. 2005 [1996]. *The Origins of the Urban Crisis: Race and Inequality in Postwar Detroit* (with a new preface by the author). Princeton, NJ: Princeton University Press.

Swartz, David L. 2002. "The Sociology of Habit: The Perspective of Pierre Bourdieu." *OTJR: Occupation, Participation and Health* 22(1 suppl): 61S–69S. https://doi.org/10.1177/153944 92020220S108.

Swidler, Ann. 2003. *Talk of Love: How Culture Matters*. Chicago, IL: University of Chicago Press.

Tajfel, Henri and Jonathan C. Turner. 1986. "The Social Identity Theory of Intergroup Behaviour," pp. 7–24 in *Psychology of Intergroup Relations*, edited by S. Worchel and W. G. Austin. Chicago, IL: Nelson-Hall.

Tavory, Iddo. 2016. Summoned: Identification and Religious Life in a Jewish Neighborhood. Chicago, IL: University of Chicago Press.

Taylor, Verta, and Nancy E. Whittier. 1999. "Lesbian Feminist Mobilization," pp. 169–94 in *Waves of Protest: Social Movements since the 1960s*, edited by J. Freeman and V. Johnson. Lanham, MD: Rowman & Littlefield.

Thornton, Sarah. 1996. *Club Cultures: Music, Media, and Subcultural Capital*. Hanover, NH: University Press of New England.

Trubetzkoy, Nikolaj, and Roman Jakobson. 1975. *N. S. Trubetzkoy's Letters and Notes*. The Hague: Mouton.

Turkle, Sherry. 1997. *Life on the Screen: Identity in the Age of the Internet*. New York: Touchstone.

Turner, Ralph. 1976. "The Real Self: From Institution to Impulse." *American Journal of Sociology* 81(5): 989–1016.

Van Dijck, José. 2013. "'You Have One Identity': Performing the Self on Facebook and LinkedIn." *Media, Culture & Society* 35(2): 199–215.

Vinitzky-Seroussi, Vered. 1998. *After Pomp and Circumstance: High School Reunion as an Autobiographical Occasion*. Chicago, IL: University of Chicago Press.

Warikoo, Natasha Kumar. 2007. "Racial Authenticity among Second Generation Youth in Multiethnic New York and London." *Poetics* 35(6): 388–408.

Waters, Mary C. 1990. *Ethnic Options: Choosing Identities in America*. Berkeley: University of California Press.

Waugh, Linda R. 1982. "Marked and Unmarked: A Choice between Unequals in Semiotic Discourse." *Semiotica* 38(3–4): 299–318.

West, Candace, and Sarah Fenstermaker. 1995. "Doing Difference." *Gender & Society* 9(1): 8–37.

West, Candace, and Don H. Zimmerman. 1987. "Doing Gender." *Gender & Society* 1(2): 125–51.

Wherry, Frederick F. 2011. *The Philadelphia Barrio: The Arts, Branding, and Neighborhood Transformation*. Chicago, IL: University of Chicago Press.

Wiebe, Robert H. 2002. *Who We Are: A History of Popular Nationalism*. Princeton, NJ: Princeton University Press.

Wilkins, Amy C. 2008. *Wannabes, Goths, and Christians: The*

Boundaries of Sex, Style, and Status. Chicago, IL: University of Chicago Press.

Williams, J. Patrick. 2006. "Authentic Identities: Straightedge Subculture, Music, and the Internet." *Journal of Contemporary Ethnography* 35(2):173–200.

Williams, J. Patrick. 2019. "Perceiving and Enacting Authentic Identities," pp. 606–22 in *The Oxford Handbook of Cognitive Sociology*, edited by W. H. Brekhus and G. Ignatow. New York: Oxford University Press.

Zerubavel, Eviatar. 1997. *Social Mindscapes: An Invitation to Cognitive Sociology*. Cambridge, MA: Harvard University Press.

Zerubavel, Eviatar. 2007. "Generally Speaking: The Logic and Mechanics of Social Pattern Analysis." *Sociological Forum* 22(2): 131–45.

Zerubavel, Eviatar. 2018. *Taken for Granted: The Remarkable Power of the Unremarkable*. Princeton, NJ: Princeton University Press.

Zerubavel, Eviatar. Forthcoming. *Generally Speaking: An Invitation to Concept-Driven Sociology*. Oxford: Oxford University Press.

Index